# ADVANCE PRAISE

"Bud's expert diagnostics were essential to my successful career change with uncanny insights to consider possibilities not yet imagined and taught me to position strengths as unassailable assets. Excellent ROI!"

—**Allison Woodward**, Director, Global Sourcing

"The Whitehouse plan for career transition is easy to follow, informative and it works. Bud is also great to work with. I highly recommend it."

—**Thomas Addison**, Sales Executive

"This book will help you get a better job. It will also help you keep it or continue upward. But if you pay attention it will do much more than that. Bud doesn't just teach job search skills. He teaches life skills. Not a day goes by that I don't use something Bud taught me."

—**Charles Wayland**, Healthcare Executive

"Since I began working with Bud, every position I have accepted has been better than the previous one, and has continually advanced my career, my finances, and my life. When I look back at the position I was in when I began to work with Bud as compared to where I am now, I do not see how I could have achieved the success I have had without him. At every crucial moment in my career since, I have relied on Bud's advice and recommendations to make the best choice possible."

—**Mark Ferraro**, Consulting Director

"Simply stated, Bud Whitehouse is the best. His 30 years in employment offer insights matched by few. Gifted in his timing, style and articulation, Bud's presentation is comprehensive, yet easily understood. His technique, his spontaneity, and subtle humor produce results. Bud educates and motivates with the best. No, he is the best."

—**Allan Libby**, Director of Tourism and Public Information

"Bud Whitehouse makes a strong claim in this book when he writes "*You will recoup your investment from the purchase of this book many times over, and you will have control, not only over your job search, but over your career, if you do what it says. Those who have understood and embraced these concepts you're about to learn have dramatically improved not just their career prospects, but their lives. You can, too.*" Strong stuff, but true. I know, because his method worked for me and I have seen it work for others many times since then. It's true for three reasons: First, Bud knows his stuff, he's been doing it for over thirty years. Second, he tells it straight, pulling no punches and revealing the tricks of his trade. And third, he wants you to succeed, not him, he cares about you and he is writing this book from his heart as well as his head. Now I am a Jew and Bud a Christian. Jews look at what folks do. I know Bud not only believes his gospel but he practices it. When he told me he helps folks at his church with finding work and does it gratis, I told him I wanted to do this for my congregations. He came along and helped me create the program, also gratis. Bud's the real deal and he and this book will help you get them to say, 'When can you start?'"

—**Robert "Bob" Rovin**sky, Principal, Consulting Firm

"I have sent everyone I have encountered these past 25 years who is in need of career help to Bud Whitehouse. He knows the field like no one else and his accumulated wisdom along with his outstanding people skills ensure the best possible results for each and every one of them. I have never had anyone tell me they were disappointed that I steered them to Bud. He is as close to a sure thing as you can find in the field."

**—Rev. Dr. David "Tuck" Knupp**

"Many people are unemployed, underemployed, or miserably employed. If you are one of these, this book is for you.

I wish I had been able to give my students this book when I worked at my last 3 universities. College graduates (and some of their parents) need Bud's wisdom and knowledge.

It is not easy to find work that you love, are good at, and that serves the world. This book will help you do that.

Bud is a professional, natural wordsmith, so this book is a delight to read. He has a natural sense of humor that gives hope to the most frustrated job seeker.

Bud is a Master Coach and I know because he coached me! Bud was my very first career coach. He taught me how to-

- Establish long range goals, identify needs, research
- Focus on a realistic position, commitment to a course of action
- Write an effective resume
- Obtain the interview and engage in stimulating conversation
- Negotiate salary and benefits without fear of mistakes
- Convert interviews to job offers to launch a brilliant career

The clients that Bud and I coached together averaged a 28% salary increase and completed their career search in just 4.7 months. 95% of the clients we worked with sent us glowing, ecstatic thank you notes.

Navigating the career world is both an art and a science. There is no captain I would rather have navigate my ship than Bud Whitehouse. Bud takes a lifetime of working as a professional career coach to inform his writing.

Do you want to leave your mark on the world?

Are you the kind of person who makes their own path?

Do you want to take responsibility for your future?

Your destiny awaits. Read and get the tools you need to shape your career.

I predict that you will be giving this book as gifts to those you love.

Work is not what one does to live, but what one lives to do. Bud's wisdom can help make this a reality."

—**Cynthia Knupp**, MA

When Can You Start?

# WHEN CAN YOU START?

## THE INSIDER'S GUIDE TO JOB SEARCH AND CAREER SUCCESS

## BUD WHITEHOUSE

NEW YORK

LONDON • NASHVILLE • MELBOURNE • VANCOUVER

# When Can You Start?

## The Insider's Guide to Job Search and Career Success

© 2020 Bud Whitehouse

Published in New York, New York, by Morgan James Publishing. Morgan James is a trademark of Morgan James, LLC. www.MorganJamesPublishing.com

ISBN 9781642797497 paperback
ISBN 9781642797503 eBook
ISBN 9781642797510 audio
Library of Congress Control Number: 2019948189

**Cover Design by:**
Christopher Kirk
www.GFSstudio.com

**Interior Design by:**
Chris Treccani
www.3dogcreative.net

Morgan James is a proud partner of Habitat for Humanity Peninsula and Greater Williamsburg. Partners in building since 2006.

Get involved today! Visit
MorganJamesPublishing.com/giving-back

To my past employers, who unwittingly taught me, to my mentor and friend Walt Limbach, who believed in me, to my wife, whose belief and support surpass human understanding, and to all my past and present clients, who have helped me learn my trade. As a surgeon once told me shortly before my operation, "You know, every day's a school day;" and finally, to God, who stuck me in jobs I didn't like, forced me to learn, and then freed me to help others.

# TABLE OF CONTENTS

# FOREWORD

I remember when Bud first shared his dream of writing this book. For decades he had assisted hundreds and hundreds of clients, one at a time, in preparing for and finding that perfect job. He said, "I want to write a book that can serve thousands of people in getting through this gauntlet without suffering unnecessary pain and anxiety. I want to show them the secrets and help them find success sooner."

It sounded like a great idea for a book. He was, after all, the authority on the topic, but writing a book is a huge undertaking.

I also remember the day I got the email. "Here is the first draft. Would you please read it?" Please understand, most people who tell me they are going to write a book, never do. Excited, I jumped in and consumed its contents. From page one to the last page it was clear, Bud had done it!

Every day, thousands of individuals post their resumés in online sites hoping to be noticed or, in response to a posted opening, submit their resumé hoping to be selected for an interview. There are few who are lucky enough to be selected, and far fewer who find success.

Then comes this masterpiece, *When Can You Start?* This book will challenge your paradigm. You will begin to see this journey from a new vantage point. Instead of being mired in the mess, you will begin to get much needed clarity.

Bud will assist you in defining your primary selling proposition—why someone should hire you. You will see your resumé differently and as a powerful tool with sharp edges that can cut through red tape. You will learn how to be more productive in your search, how to network more effectively, interview more authentically, negotiate from a position of strength and ultimately secure that new and exciting job—and then be more successful than you have in the past.

This is not a book about theory. Contained in these pages are decades of hard-won knowledge, based on the experiences of thousands of clients, as well as Bud's own lifetime of involvement in employment. These tools work.

Hundreds have paid thousands of dollars for these secrets. Now they are yours for the cost of a book and a good evening of reading. But please don't minimize Bud's advice because you did not pay him $10,000. This book is a gift from Bud to you. Please treasure it.

Are you ready to dig in, discover the secrets, implement them with precision and ultimately find that perfect job? If so, let's get started. Turn the page and begin the journey by changing the way you have been thinking about the job search.

Dave Blanchard
CEO
The Og Mandino Leadership Institute

# PREFACE

I *had* to write this book.

I've never met a soul who truly enjoyed looking for a job. More typical is the client who recognized well in advance that his Fortune-ranked employer would fail, but stayed until the very bitter end because the mere *thought* of having to look for another job was so distasteful.

Why is this?

The lack of control resulting from ignorance about how to get a job seems to be primary. After all, most people don't look for a job often enough to become truly competent. Most seem to get jobs the way I did back in the day—by wandering around the employment marketplace until something happened to me.

That is a very expensive (and deeply depressing) way to look for a job. If you're unemployed, divide your last salary by 52; this represents the opportunity cost per week of your job search. It doesn't take long to realize that ignorance is costing you a lot. If you're still employed, consider the fact that, having emotionally left your employer, it won't be easy to focus on the job or hide a job search.

Once they've gotten the job, many people forget everything they can about the job search, turn their careers over to their employer, and relax, unaware that their employer is staying up late at night, looking for a way to succeed without them. In today's work environment it's likely that within three years a change will occur to cause you to have to look for another job, so turning over your career to your employer is no longer an option.

Whether you are a boomer, and the millennials are gaining on you, or a millennial coping in what is still, in large part, a boomer's world, ignorance is not your friend.

If you can relate to any or all of this, it is my hope and expectation that this book will be the answer for you. Getting a job and managing a career aren't random acts. Like any other activity, they involve developing a knowledge of what to do, how to do it, and a set of skills that brings results. Is it fun? Not so much. Is it effective? *Very.*

Consider this book (and me) a personal guide, teaching you what to do, how to do it, and helping you develop the mindset and skills to succeed. One step at a time it will show you what to sell on a resumé and in an interview, how to document it, how to network effectively (*i.e.*, not asking people to do your job search for you), how to turn an interview into a conversation enabling you to be seen as the answer to a problem, not as just another future problem, the secret of interview follow-up, how to negotiate an offer, and what to do in the new job to guarantee success.

Let's get started.

# ACKNOWLEDGMENTS

I owe an enormous debt of gratitude to Constance Costas, a fierce editor, benevolent and wise coach, and good friend, without whom this book may never have seen the light of day, as well as to David Hancock, Bonnie Rauch, and the rest of the team at Morgan-James Publishing, who do so well the mysterious work of which I am so startlingly and painfully ignorant, and who had faith in me and my ability to write something worth reading.

# INTRODUCTION

> *"The great enemy of the truth is very often*
> *not the lie . . . but the myth"*
> **– JOHN F. KENNEDY**

I have a friend, a sports psychologist, who says that finding a job in the 21$^{st}$ century is like going on national television to play a sport you haven't played for ten years—that you weren't even good at ten years ago.

Most people can readily identify with this. In more than 30 years in all aspects of employment, I've only met one person who enjoyed looking for a job ("Bud, I know if I keep doing this, I'm going to get a great job, but I'm going to miss talking to all these *wonderful* people!"). It's worse than having to play a sport you don't play well. It's like playing one you've never played before when you don't even know the rules!

## Fear

Yes, fear is the reason people feel this way. For many, a job search takes you into the great unknown, forces you to go beyond your comfort zone, to be vulnerable when you don't want to be, and, it seems, to be the world's foremost authority when you're not even sure that your knowledge is adequate. When you think about it like that, it's scary. But it doesn't have to be that way. If you need a mortgage, you go to a mortgage specialist. If you have a legal problem, you go to an attorney. You find the expert. But when it's time to find a job, many think you're on your own.

Not so. Job hunting and career management simply involve developing a skill set, and I will teach you that skill set. It may not be easy for you. It will involve your changing certain ways you may currently look at things, and, yes, you will sometimes have to be vulnerable when, as one client put it, "You realize this goes against every fiber in my being, don't you?" (her job search was successful). But after a successful job search, you will marvel at your new abilities, and the freedom they give you. Another client told me, "Bud, you don't teach just job hunting skills. You teach *life* skills."

A brief word about me. When I talk to groups, I always seem to intimidate a few people. I'm big and I have a sarcastic, sometimes obscure sense of humor. It is definitely not my intent to intimidate you in this book, but rather, to partner with you. But if you do find me a little scary on occasion, I can assure you it will be nothing like the scariness of an interview you haven't prepared for, or a hiring manager asking your weaknesses, and holding your feet to the fire. My goal is to make the unknown of the job hunting process known, and to coach you to success through an increased knowledge base and the ability to use that knowledge in an impactful way.

## Myths

Most people looking for a job seem to follow a set of rules. They:

1. spend hours every day filling out applications and sending resumés online;
2. scour online classified sites;
3. look for headhunters to do the heavy lifting, if they will;
4. network with friends, relatives, colleagues, and strangers.

I wish I could tell you this works, but I've seen way too many people walk in the door, who have done these things for months with nothing to show for it but extreme frustration. Maybe you can relate to these folks, and maybe, like them, you have begun to wonder what's wrong with you. Or maybe you're just totally frustrated. Here's the good news. You are not the problem. The method is the problem. I will show you a better way.

## Stability

You've been shaken by a job loss, or you just want another, better, job. This is where most people start getting in trouble. Their first thought is that they need an employer who is going to be around for a while. Stability is critical since they're getting older and will need a retirement.

The problem is there is no such thing as a stable company—large or small—today. The one thing you can count on is instability—frequent, sudden change being the rule of the day. Technology, the advent of a global marketplace, and the way company management now views employees have combined to dramatically change the way we look at jobs and careers.

The idea that the larger the company, the more stable proved to be a misnomer as far back as the 1980s. Since our most recent recession, 2007 to 2009, General Motors, arguably the largest, most Blue Chip company since the 1950s, declared bankruptcy. Companies with fewer than 200 employees have provided the greatest number of new jobs in the last forty years. Amazon started out in Jeff Bezos's garage.

The fact that change is upon us and moving ever faster is threatening to most people. But, as you read this book, I hope you will see that in reality change is your friend. All change creates opportunity.

But no company will hire you.

An *individual* will hire you. And that person will hire you not to fill a vacancy, but because they believe you can solve their problem. All hiring is done to solve problems.

As an employer, if I have no problems, I certainly won't spend money hiring someone. That's just common sense. And what it means to you is this: you are not looking for a company with a vacancy. You're looking for a person with a problem. This is a critical difference because of the way jobs are filled.

## The Internet

In 2000, roughly one in six jobs was filled through newspaper classified sections, headhunters, and the internet. Today most newspaper classified sections have been replaced with online versions, headhunters are still around, and the internet has exploded.

If we conservatively assume the internet has tripled in its presence, it now increases those statistics from one in six jobs to one in two. But that's one in two vacancies. Here's the problem: many jobs were never vacancies.

The actual percentage doesn't lend itself easily to measurement. I have read that the percentage of jobs that weren't vacancies ranges from 35 to 85 percent, depending on whom you want to believe. My own experience tells me the actual number is closer to 35 percent. But even if you accept 35 percent as the number, this tells you that only 65% of all jobs, at most, were ever vacancies. Those that weren't? They were problems until the right person walked in. And then they were jobs. But they were never vacancies. I've seen this played out in companies ranging from the Fortune 500 to start-ups with fewer than 10 employees.

But this isn't an accurate picture of things. If the internet and headhunters fill only one half of vacancies, you're losing 50 percent of the vacancy market by spending hours on line and praying for a headhunter to rescue you. Add that 32.5 percent to the 35 percent of jobs that were never vacancies, and in reality you've lost *two thirds* of the marketplace. Even if the internet and headhunters filled *all* the vacancies, you've still lost 35 percent of the market. If I were to cut your pay, or your food intake, or your time away from work by 35 percent, you would hate me! And the piece of the market that you may be looking at is the same tired fraction that everyone else in the world is searching. Hence, maximum competition.

In the March 2009 edition of *Smart Money*, Anne Kadet describes applying online.

---

*Applying for a position increasingly involves two phases. Step one: Use the employer's online application center to submit your carefully-crafted resumé and cover letter. Step two: Sit and wait until the sun burns out and your bones turn to dust. Recruiters say that the percentage of online applications viewed by an actual human being ranges from 5 to 25 percent.*

---

Of course, this applies primarily to large companies with budgets big enough to buy the software that is so efficient at ruling you out. In small companies, virtually every resumé that comes in is seen by a human—for about ten seconds.

## Headhunters

Let's discuss headhunters for a moment. I was one for too long. A headhunter is someone who places people in companies and collects a fee from the employer. (There are still people out there who will charge you if they place you, but they are mercifully few, and you should avoid them.) They vary from the large international firms like Korn Ferry to local mom and pop employment agencies. Though the people at Korn Ferry will hate me, for simplicity I'll call them all headhunters. Headhunters can be very useful to you if you are in an easily defined job and looking for the next rung on the ladder. If not, you are not the headhunter's friend.

Headhunters are paid by the employer. This tells you that the employer is the client, not you. To the headhunter, you are either gold or dirt. You are gold if you meet an employer's specifications, and the employer is interested in you. Rejoice if this happens. But you will revert to dirt the moment the employer loses interest. Headhunters are infamous for not returning phone calls, but you shouldn't take it personally. To the headhunter time is money, and if you are repeatedly calling, you are wasting both of his. He'll call if he has something to tell you. All this said, I've had clients who have maintained long term relationships with headhunters, and benefitted accordingly.

## Networking

The vacancy/problem statistics seem to leave networking as the most viable tool to find a job. But this is how America networks. We go to everyone we know, and many we don't, and ask them to put their reputations and trusted or reporting relationships at risk for us. This doesn't work well. And when it doesn't, we back up and do it all over again, just harder. Is it any wonder that after a while our friends start avoiding us?

I expect you've already concluded that this kind of thing won't help, but these are the rules many tend to play by when they need to find a job. Why? Because this is what we have been taught and is ingrained in us from an early age.

The problem is that these are the wrong rules. There is a better way. You will recoup your investment from the purchase of this book many times over, and you will have control, not only over your job search, but over your career, if you do what it says. Those who have understood and embraced these concepts you're about to learn have dramatically improved not just their career prospects, but their lives. You can, too.

# CHAPTER 1

# Changing the Way You Think

> *"Insanity: Doing the same thing over and over
> and expecting different results."*
> **– ALBERT EINSTEIN**

## Change

Change is unsettling, uncomfortable. It's human nature to resist it, especially when that change is perceived to be a threat. Sudden change is especially unsettling. Consider combat.

In Southeast Asia, in 1968, upon walking into an ambush, I found it instinctive to want to get away. The quickest way to do that was to drop to the earth and ensure there was nothing between me and the dirt but my shirt buttons. This reaction was totally intuitive.

Totally intuitive and totally fatal, because if you are lying there, the bad guys will keep shooting at you and sooner or later, they'll get you.

The correct and totally counterintuitive thing to do was to immediately turn and charge *into* the ambush. The only way to get away from the bad guys was to get them before they got you! And the only way to do that was to get up close and personal as quickly as possible. Curiously, both sides in the Civil War figured this out. Who knew?

So, how does this example relate to finding a job? Because it involves changing your way of thinking. Use what seems to be counterintuitive to change the outcome. For you, change may involve losing a job—a huge change. It always comes with a change of workmates, company culture, and responsibility. And it feels distressingly like the ambush described above—sitting in front of the hiring manager or human resources representative while they take their best shot at you.

Why talk of change? Because to be successful in this undertaking, you will have to embrace it and change certain mental habits you may have developed, perhaps unconsciously. Having grown up in the American work culture, you have been subjected to ways of thinking that may run counter to reality, and you may be blissfully unaware of it. The good news is that just about everyone else in the U.S. shares them. Once you have corrected these, you'll be ready to win.

Over the next few pages we're going to talk about the bad news, myths, several of which you might presently see as reality. This is not an attempt to scare you, although you might not enjoy some of what there is to read. Press on! After the bad news, we get to the really good news—how you can get a great job, be paid what you're worth (or more), and actually enjoy going to work, unlike more than half of the American workforce!

The first myth to work on is that you need to find a company with a vacancy. You don't. You need to find a person with a problem.

## The How & Why of Hiring

So, I have pointed out that companies don't hire—people do. And they hire to solve problems—not to fill vacancies. Let's look into this a little more deeply. Hiring is a manager's second most distasteful task—right behind firing and well ahead of performance evaluations. If they have a problem they typically have tried to use those salary dollars every other possible way first. They hire only as a last resort—they need a human being in their organization to do what no one else there can do.

If a manager likes you, and he believes you can solve his problem, you have a job—even if there was no job there when you walked in. That's just human nature. And wherever you have worked or will work, you see this behavior.

Look at it from the standpoint of the employer. Suppose he needs to hire someone. How is he going to find that person? The odds are he'll advertise. The options are limited. Along with advertising through the company website and/or conventional (print) methods, he can tell everyone he knows he's looking for someone, and he can call a headhunter. Once he's done all that, his alternatives are few. If he does advertise, he'll probably do it on the company website first.

What will the ad say?

"A degree in this, three to five years of experience in that, and blah, blah, blah." It's that word *experience* that gets everyone, including the employer, off track. And here we come to another myth, and that is that managers hire based on experience.

In an employment interview, there are three critical factors:

---

*Chemistry*—How well do you and the interviewer get along?
*Ability*—Does the interviewer believe you can do the work?
*Experience*—Have you done the work?

---

Which of these would you say is most important to the interviewer?

As you will soon see, these three are important in the order listed. Experience is the least important of the three. So why in the world is he advertising for experience?

He's doing this because he believes it is easier to evaluate experience than to evaluate ability on a resumé, and it's impossible to evaluate chemistry. When advertising a vacancy in today's economy, a company is looking at somewhere between 300 and 3,000 responses to a single ad. If the ad says, "must have the ability to do blah, blah, and blah," every one of those responses will say, "I can do blah, blah, and blah," and then where is the manager? But experience is a standard. It is measurable. So, it's experience that goes into the ad.

Now the manager has at least his first 300 responses together in a nice, neat stack.

Does he evaluate them by chemistry? No way.

Can he evaluate them by ability? Maybe, maybe not, probably not.

What about by experience? You bet!

He makes his first cut, which is in many respects the most important cut, based on the least important of the three critical factors. If you have two years of experience, and the ability to do the job, will you get an interview? No, you don't meet the experience requirement. If you have a degree in something else, or even no degree, but three years of experience doing that exact same work, will you get an interview? No, you don't meet the degree requirement. This despite the fact that as much as 90 percent of people with a bachelor's degree work in a field other than their field of study.

It is also one reason hiring is so high on a manager's avoidance list—because when the manager hires, he's at risk. He doesn't like being at risk.

Let's say you need to hire someone.

You have three people standing in front of you. In most respects, they appear equal, but one came through your website, one was referred to you by someone you know and trust, and one *is* someone you know and trust. Which one do you want to hire?

The one you know and trust. Why? Because that person is a known quantity. There is almost no risk associated with hiring this person.

Second, the person who was referred to you by someone you know and trust. Why? Because that person, while not necessarily a known quantity, is at least known by a known quantity. You have some risk associated with hiring this person, but that risk is mitigated by the relationship that got him/her in front of you.

That leaves the person who came through the ad. No one wants this one. Why? Because you are totally at risk in hiring this unknown. This is why managers take valued subordinates with them from job to job.

Let's suppose that person is no longer available. Now whom do you want to hire?

So, an intelligent employer who has a need but doesn't know of someone to hire will first ask his professional friends and acquaintances who they know who might be available. Only failing that will the employer go to the company website, the headhunter, or a job board to advertise.

If all this weren't discouraging enough, in responding to an ad, you are trying to fit your identity into a job that wasn't designed with you in mind. Does this mean you should disregard the web, headhunters, or the classifieds? No. They still represent a part of the marketplace too big to ignore. You'll be using all these methods but perhaps in a different way than you thought.

### Networking: The Three Deadly Sins

I once saw a bumper sticker that said, *Networking is Notworking.* It was right. The way people typically network does not work.

### Networking Scenario #1

I'm your friend. You come to me and say, "Bud, who do you know with a job? I need to get a job!" Perhaps I know that my friend, Bob, has a problem. I say, "Well, you ought to speak with my friend, Bob. Maybe he'll hire you." You go see Bob, and he does hire you. But you don't work out, so Bob fires you. Now, that's a problem for you, for sure. But is that a problem for me? You bet it is. Who do you think Bob is going to blame? Himself? No way. Bob is normal. He's going to blame me!

Fortunately for me, I knew of that potential long before you ever showed up. So, when you ask, "Who do you know with a job?" I say, "Gee, I don't know. But let me keep my ear to the ground. You'll be the first to hear of anything I hear about." Then you'll try to get me to take your resumé. If you're a typical friend, what you just heard me say is, "I'm going to look for a job for you." You should probably not stray too far away from the phone, because surely, I'll be calling. But that's not what I said. What I said was code for, "You're a nice person, I hope you find a job. I'm really trying to show support for you, but I will never be caught in the same room alone with you again." And what will I do with your resumé? I'll do one of two things with it. I'll say, "I'll be sure to give this to Human Resources." What do you think will happen to it in Human Resources? Yes—it will die a cold and lonely death.

Or, with the best of intentions, I'll take it home and lay it down somewhere until I figure out what to do with it. Then I will forget it. Three months from now, I'll trip over it and throw it away—several weeks after the end of our friendship. To you, I'm no longer your friend. I gave you no help at all. And now it looks like I'm trying to avoid you. And you are correct.

What you are asking me to do here is sponsor you for a job. That involves my being willing to take a risk, that is, to risk my relationship with someone I know, perhaps a superior, to get you a job. Human nature dictates that I won't do that.

The simple fact is that no one likes looking for a job. Just as the employer puts off hiring because of the risk, most will do whatever they can to avoid it, including turning their search over to anyone who looks like they'll take responsibility for it. The problem with this is that no one else will take responsibility for your job search. You're going to have to do it. Hopefully, it was that realization that caused you to buy this book.

Never try to hand off responsibility for your job search to someone else. No one will take it. There is no one more motivated than you to find you a job, and soon, no one more knowledgeable about how to do that than you.

## Networking Scenario #2

It's a beautiful Saturday morning, and you're driving down the road. On the side of the road, there is a broken-down car with a non-threatening person standing beside it. Your first thought is, "I should help this person." Your next thought is, "Gee, I really need to get to the grocery store." So, you drive on.

Your personal busy-ness kept you from going out of your way to help another person. Well, we're all too busy. And my busy-ness always takes precedence over your job search.

## Networking Scenario #3

Assume you and I are talking. You seem like a nice person, and I'd like to help you. In the warm fuzziness of the moment, I'll make a commitment to do something on your behalf. We then go our separate ways, and two hours later, I'm asking myself, "Why did you say you would do that? You knew it was wishful thinking when you said it. You knew it wouldn't work." And so, I won't do what I said I would do. Do I tell you I'm not going to do what I said I would do? No, I'll just avoid you in the future.

People will not take a risk, and they won't go out of their way. Some will violate the principle of making a commitment to do something for you. Most of the time they will also break the commitment.

These are the Three Deadly Sins of Networking. By trying to cause people to go out of their way, take a risk, or make a commitment to do something, you practically guarantee that they won't help you. This is nothing more than human nature at work.

But by the same token, if you allow people to help you without going out of their way, or taking a risk, or making a commitment to do something for you, they'll help you in a heartbeat, and feel better about themselves for doing it—because deep down, we all like to help people. We just don't like to pay a price for it.

By recognizing human nature and making it work for you, you will find success. Everyone else will be trying to overcome it the way our culture says we should.

## The Interview

Earlier I talked about the major factors in an interview—chemistry, ability, and experience. Let's unpack this a little more thoroughly, because your understanding of this dynamic is critical.

## Chemistry

Chemistry is the most important. It's very simple, really. If the interviewer doesn't like you, they won't care how good you are. You're not getting hired. If they do like you, you are well on your way to getting hired.

## Ability vs Experience

Look at it this way. If the interviewer likes you and believes you're capable of doing the job, how much do they care if you haven't done it before? They can give you the experience, but not the ability. Ability always trumps experience in the interview. Incongruous, right? That's not to say experience is unimportant. It's one of three critical factors. But of the three, it is the least important. If you are just graduating from college, changing careers, or reaching for the logical next step on the career ladder, this should make you feel better.

This becomes good news, because your competition is trying to sell themselves based on their experience, and they're in big trouble. It's questionable that the hiring manager may relate to their experience, but he or she can easily relate to your ability.

Earlier I said that about 35 percent of jobs were never vacancies; they were problems until the right person walked in. I also said people get jobs primarily by informal means. That is a big percentage. Believe it. I see it happen all the time. But I also believe that of those who find a job by informal means, many do it by accident. I am an example.

I've had seven jobs in my career. Every job I found, I found by informal means. I got two on purpose. I set out using what I knew to get what I wanted. One search took three days, the other took ten days. The other five jobs I got the way most people get them. I wandered around the employment landscape until something happened to me. Those searches took as long as a year.

---

*Recognize how human nature works,*
*and take advantage of it.*

---

## Create Your Job

You may do a job search the way our culture says to do it, and you might end up getting one because you twisted your identity into the shape of that job description better than anyone else, or you can go create a job that fits you. How do you do this? By becoming a known quantity before there is a need.

Whether you call it the informal process, the referral process, networking, or any other name, it's the way most people get jobs, and it's what I'm going to teach you. According to surveys, as much as 40 percent who use this method create the jobs they take. How do they do that?

## The Life Cycle Of a Job

You may have played a role in a situation like this, wittingly or not, but it's not what most people think about when it's time to get a job. (Diagram follows)

A. I, the VP of Finance, hire someone. Life is good. I had a problem, but now I've got someone to take care of that. I can go on with my own job.

B. Life is not as good as I thought. My new employee, Goober Smokebreak, isn't meeting my expectations, or is working far above my expectations—that's a problem, too. Or there could be other possible problems.

C. I'm in crisis! Smokebreak is an idiot! There is no question that he'll fail, and he'll be gone. But what happens when they start asking, "Who's the idiot who hired the idiot?"

D. D really occurs immediately after C. Goober is history as soon as I can make it happen. So, what does it take to do this job right? Now, I'm mentally defining Goober's replacement.

E. I fire Goober, or my superstar gives notice. Now I have a whole new problem.

Those who want Goober's job, have two problems. First, 299 other people want this job. What's the statistical likelihood that any one of them look better on paper than those 299 others do? Second, this job is now in hardened concrete—I've written a position description. Those who want the job must twist their identities into this shape. The person who does that best wins. So they have maximum competition and must look like the job. But here's the secret to job hunting success.

If you come see me anywhere between point **A** and point **E**, you have no competition, and you can make the job look like you.

Come see me between points **A** and **B**, and my reaction is, "I like you. I don't have a need right now, but let me hang onto your resumé." And your resumé goes into the file I keep in my desk, on my computer, or in my head, for future hires.

See me between points **B** and **D** and I'll say, "Let's talk!"

See me between points **D** and **E** and my response is, "Let me hang onto your resumé so I can write a position description!"

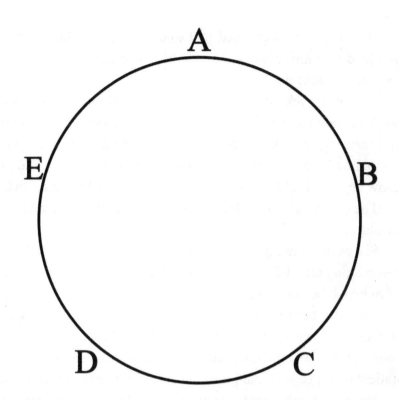

You've heard of the hidden marketplace or the unpublished marketplace? This is it.

Most job-seekers are focusing on the vacancy, point **E** to point **A**. That's around a quarter of the market. **A** through **D** is the other three quarters.

So where do you want to be?

If you aren't looking in 100 percent of the job market, you have a problem. But your focus should be on points **A** through **D**, not **E** to **A**.

Years ago, I worked with a client who was being fired. After a meeting one day, I said to him, "For our next meeting, I want you to write down the names of everyone you know who you think could help you in a job search."

He moaned and groaned and told me this wouldn't work, that he didn't know anyone. I told him to give it a try, and I'd see him the next week.

The next week, he had six names written down. I said, "No, no. You didn't get it. I wanted you to write down the names of *everyone* you know who you think could help you." He complained again and told me this wouldn't work, that he didn't know anyone. I told him to try again, and I'd see him in a week.

The next week, he had the same six names. So, that's where we started.

Six weeks later, he had a new job doing what he loved and was making about 20 percent more than he had been in the job from which he was being fired. And he had a file of 350 names.

This guy became my personal research project. I followed him for five years. During that time, he stayed in touch with about 25 of those people. And the number was dynamic, not static. Some people would drop out and others would be added.

He consistently sent these people birthday cards. If he saw a magazine article, a book, or a newspaper article he thought one of them might enjoy, he sent it to them. Once or twice in a year, he would call and say, "Let's get together for dinner and catch up." If one of these people was looking for a job, he would knock himself out to help.

In the five years that I followed him, he was recruited for two more jobs with substantial increases in salary each time. He didn't go looking for these jobs. Each was the result of a phone call from one of these people to whom he was so attentive. He would be happily doing his job when one of them would call and say, "You might want to have a look at what's going on over here," which turned out to be code for, "Please accept this job we have designed for you!"

That is a better way to get a job than what you're dealing with right now!

Here is the incentive for you:

---

*If you do this right one time,
you will never have to do it again!*

---

This isn't to say that getting a job is an easy process, or that it doesn't require effort. On the contrary, it requires a lot of effort, and it doesn't stop when you get a job.

When in your forties, you're probably looking at working another twenty years, plus or minus. In today's economy, that equates to another six or seven jobs. In your thirties, add three or more jobs to that. In your twenties, don't bother counting. Today's work culture guarantees that the company you work for will experience bankruptcy, be bought by another company, will buy another company, or change its way of doing business. Technology will change, your boss will change, what you do will be transferred offshore at a drastically reduced pay rate, or something else will happen that will cause you to have to find another job. In today's economy, this will likely happen within three years.

You remember Goober. You're going to see Goober often. He's the guy who just can't get it right. He believes that if he does his work well, he will be noticed and rewarded. This is a myth. In today's employment environment, if you do your work well, you will be noticed and kept in the same job until you are no longer needed, unless you know how to manage your career. You can face what you're facing now six to ten or more times, or you can do the search right once, and manage your career afterword. We'll talk about that later..

So let's summarize:

## Reality (THE BAD NEWS)

1. The website vacancy is as it seems—a black hole. By responding to the ad, you are competing with the entire population of people who saw the ad while they were looking for a company with a vacancy— those 300 to 3,000 mentioned earlier, many with specific industry or technical experience that you may lack.
2. The headhunter isn't on your side. They're being paid by the potential employer, so it is the employer who is the client. The headhunter controls the search, and thereby, your career. We'll talk more about this later.
3. The company won't hire you—a person will—and that person may not even have a vacancy until you become the solution to his problem.
4. In the unlikely event that you do get an interview from the website application, or if you get one through the headhunter, you are the employer's greatest risk, and possibly his worst nightmare! His job, as you will see later, becomes to find out what's wrong with you so he doesn't have to hire you.
5. Networking in the typical way will not get you a job. It will lose friends.
6. The HR representative is trying to rule you out.

## Reality (THE GOOD NEWS)

1. By talking with people the right way instead of spending 6 hours a day online looking for a job, you will be successful.
2. There is nothing wrong with working with a headhunter, except depending on him/her.
3. A person, not a company, will hire you. Focusing on this fact drastically increases your chance of getting a great job.
4. If you sit before the hiring manager when they're not hiring, you can develop a relationship, the manager can like you, see you as the answer to a present or future problem, and hire you.
5. Networking the right way will expand your social capital and get you a great job.
6. The HR representative will always try to rule you out. The hiring manager won't, if he/she is approached in the right way.
7. If you conduct the search the right way, you can create a great job for yourself, or modify an existing job to more comfortably fit you.

# CHAPTER 2
## What Do You Have to Sell?

> "... *the value of experience is overrated, usually by old men who nod wisely and speak stupidly.*"
> **Scroll 1, The Greatest Salesman in the World**
> **—OG MANDINO**

I've been harping on the fact that you are selling a set of abilities, not your experience. Actually, what you are selling is success using a set of abilities.

If an employer likes you and believes you're *capable* of doing the work, he won't care that you haven't done the work. You're probably really tired of reading that, but it is a concept that is critical to success. And I'm not saying he'll train you, because he doesn't want to do that. Training costs money.

Here's the point. If you have no experience doing the work, but you have experience successfully using the skills required for the work, an employer should expect you to be successful doing the work. What you lack is not ability, but environmental knowledge, which can be gained on the job. There are exceptions, as in my case, when the surgeon said to me, "You know, every day is a school day," three days before operating on me. I knew that, but didn't really want to hear it from him!

It is of critical importance to understand the difference. When changing careers and trying to sell your experience, you're in trouble. Many of those potential employers who might hire you lack that experience themselves and are unable to relate to your experience. If you're trying to sell it and they can't understand it, they're not buying it. Moreover, as noted, experience is not a guarantee of ability. You must be able to tell a prospective employer how you can help them make or save money in terms they can understand.

Now it's time to do some heavy lifting. If you're going to be selling your skills, it will be helpful to know what they are. Note that when I refer to skills, I'm not talking about technology- or industry-specific skills. I'm talking about garden variety, generic abilities, like developing relationships, leading others, etc.

Over the next couple of pages, I have provided a list of six abilities that, at minimum, you had better be able to sell if you want to be successful in the search. But you have many more abilities than these. Yours might include establishing systems and procedures, persuading, negotiating, managing things (processes, not people), coordinating, directing, writing, training, leading others, team building, mentoring, presenting, conceptualizing, initiating, persevering, and on, and on. The list is practically endless. Note that these all show up as action verbs.

The easiest way to identify some of yours if you don't have help is to identify achievements from work. If you're a new grad, you can also use volunteer efforts, summer jobs, or school. If you're changing careers, use work if you can, but, if necessary, you can use volunteer experience. Next, break down how you achieved them using action verbs like the ones above. I've given you six skills that you must sell, but you should easily be able to come up with at least six more.

Here's the hard part. If you follow my guidance above and wind up with twelve abilities, including the six I've given you, you are going to have to identify thirty-six examples of success (three examples for each skill), to prove successful use of these skills. For the sake of guidance, I have assumed that you only identified six more skills than I gave you. This will not be fun, but it will get you a great job. Put in the effort. This is some of the most important work you will do.

If you are not a new grad or changing careers, only work-related achievements count. You must have been paid to do it. The person who will hire you will relate much better to work than to anything else.

Clients call this The Homework from Hell. The reason is that you must go back through your entire work history to identify these successes, so if you have more than about five years of experience, you are going to spend considerable parts of the next forty-eight hours swearing at me.

Learn from this. If you have been documenting success in real time, this is easy. But most people, including Goober, haven't and won't do that, and they pay dearly for it when it's time to do a resumé or interview for a job. Goober thinks it's his boss's job to notice his success. But he's wrong, and thankfully you are not Goober. If you didn't document success before, now you know to do it every week of your working life after this, recognizing that your boss most likely won't. The pain you're going through now is an investment in your working future.

This is the essence of career management. We'll talk about this in detail in the last chapter.

The easiest way to do this assignment is to invest considerable effort in identifying successes. Then see which skills they fit most easily with. Sitting there and asking yourself, "How have I created success by leading others?" will most likely just give you a headache. Keep in mind that you don't have to change the world with the achievement. You are simply documenting success using a skill.

Let's get started. Here are my six:

You are of value to an employer to the degree that you can convince him that you are able to set goals and objectives, plan for their achievement, organize and manage work or work teams, analyze situations and make solid decisions addressing them, solve problems, and manage money.

Let's look at these one at a time. *NOTE*: You would do well to read through the rest of this chapter before starting work.

## Setting Goals and Objectives

Setting goals and objectives is something every company in America does. Some do it more formally than others, but they all do it. It is most obvious in the sales department, but it is ubiquitous. Whether you are a manager—no matter at what level—or not, this is one of your most significant responsibilities.

Example: Set and achieved a goal to increase sales.

Identify at least three examples of goals you set, as well as the objectives to achieve them, and identify the positive result you obtained.

## Planning

Planning is a daily, weekly, monthly, and annual task in a company. Identify at least three examples of planning you have done, and their successful outcomes. None of these can be an event you identified above.

Example: Planned the corporate relocation of a 500-employee company.

## Organizing Work or Work Teams

Organizing work and/or the people to perform these tasks is a critical skill, not only for a manager, but for anyone. Many managers in corporate America became managers because they were good at what they did prior to becoming managers, not because they're good managers. Identify at least three examples of your having successfully organized a work effort or organized and managed the work team that performed it. None of these can be an event you identified above.

Example: Organized a team to address overdue accounts receivable.

## Analyzing

The ability to analyze a situation quickly and accurately and determine a course of action based on your analysis will separate you from much of the rest of the herd. Your willingness to be responsible, and your developed skills of analysis and decision-making, will cause you to stand out here.

Identify at least three examples of your ability to analyze a situation and make the correct decision as to a course of action. None of these can be an event you identified above.

Example: Analyzed manufacturing processes to improve efficiency.

## Problem Solving

Problem solving just goes with the territory, because no program or project goes the way it was planned.

Identify at least three problems that you were able to solve that no one else could. None of these can be an event you identified above.

Example: Solved a staff turnover problem by improving morale.

## Budgeting

In corporate America, managing money means budgeting and/or staying within the budget.

If you haven't been responsible for a budget, don't despair. You can skip this one. Budgeting is the odd one out in this list. The other abilities are innate, but budgeting is learned behavior. It appears in this list because if you are in management you had better be able to demonstrate budget skills. If you have been responsible for budget processes or management, identify at least three examples of success. If you have managed projects with associated budgets, identify at least three examples of projects that you completed on time and within budget. None of these can be an event you identified above.

Example: Completed the year within budget, despite the addition of three major unplanned projects.

To give structure to these, each example should be composed of three parts.

1. What you did
2. The specific steps you took, using action words
3. The quantified beneficial result for your employer

Pay attention to the third part. The result must be in terms of increased revenue, reduced cost, increased production, productivity, or efficiency, first ever, biggest or smallest—some standard of measure. It must also, to the degree possible, be specifically in terms of dollars or percentage.

---

*The result must be beneficial to your employer; not to you.*

---

If you tell me you increased organizational efficiency, and I'm inclined to be at all hostile, I'll ask myself, "by how much—one percent?" But if you tell me you increased organizational efficiency by 17 percent, I'm impressed on two levels. First, I'm impressed with the percentage. Second, I'm impressed that you know the percentage.

## Success Story

*Sentence 1: What did you do?*

> Imported products directly from China that had previously been sourced through wholesalers.

*Sentence 2: How did you do it?*

> Wrote product specs, requested samples from multiple Chinese factories to test quality and compliance, selected factories, negotiated pricing, arranged for overseas shipping, and traveled to China to meet with factory principals.

*Sentence 3: What was the result?*

> Increased gross margin on selected products by 120 percent.

Now, here's a problem many of my clients have had. When communicating, we do so from pictures in our heads. We do not see words—we see events. We also typically communicate from within the context of what we see. But the hiring manager or the reader of your resumé or profile wasn't present at the event you're describing and cannot see inside your head. You must describe it from his point of view, not yours.

Example:

1.  Improved the company's retention rate.
2.  Conducted focus groups to determine employee issues, blah blah blah, developed and implemented policies and procedures to address the issues.
3.  Reduced employee turnover to 10 percent.

Now, on its face, this isn't so bad. But Goober didn't give the event any context. I, the reader, don't know, and can't guess, the scale of the problem. Suppose, in his first sentence, Goober had said, "Solved the problem of employee turnover averaging 40 percent. Now a reduction to 10 percent means something. It could also be stated as a 75 percent reduction in the turnover rate.

This is some of the most important and difficult work you will do to prepare for a job search. The product of this exercise will be used in two ways. First, it will make up part of your resumé. Second, these are answers to an interviewer's question of, "Tell me about a time when you had a situation like this. Tell me what you did about it, and the result you achieved."

This is called a behavioral question. Behavioral questions are very popular, the theory being that what you have done before, you will do again.

If you can develop twenty-five to fifty success stories, you will never have a problem with this kind of question.

I'm guessing you won't have much fun with this effort. Again,

*Learn from this!*

If you aren't like Goober, you won't share Goober's problems. Successful career management includes keeping a record of those successes, both for performance evaluations and for future job searches. If you haven't been doing this, start today.

## Passion

You have been hard at work identifying and writing about your successes. This is good, but did you enjoy them? And by enjoy, I mean not just the result, but the use of the skill set, the process. As long as you did, you won't be setting yourself up for an unpleasant future.

After working in human resources for a few years, I found myself interviewing for an HR position with an up-and-coming computer manufacturer, a great opportunity at the time. I could give you several examples of success in my HR experience, but the truth is I had absolutely no passion for the work. I had no idea what else I might do—I was an HR guy. I must have known subconsciously that I shouldn't pursue it though, because I watched myself in wonder (and horror) as I sabotaged myself in the interview. Thank heaven I did! The worst thing that could have happened to me would have been getting that job!

This is something you really need to ponder. Perhaps you're thinking that you don't know what it is that you want to do. If you don't, this book will help you find it. It's my experience that many people who say they don't know what they want to do, do know, but are afraid to say so.

Years ago, I had a client who had been a customer service representative, and had not fared well in his career. In our first meeting, I asked him what he wanted to do. His eyes lit up, he leaned forward, and passionately explained that it would be great to be a sales representative. When he said this, my first thought was, "No way." From my point of view, he was missing several attributes that might make him a successful sales rep and had some that could get in his way. But I had learned by then not to tell the client that his dream was impossible.

Several meetings later, as we were approaching the search, I asked him again, "What do you want to do?" He told me he thought he should be in customer service. I said, "That's not what you told me before."

He said, "What did I tell you?"

I responded, "You told me you wanted to be a sales representative."

At this point he started backing away from me, and stuttering, "Oh, but I, uh, but . . .."

I asked, "Do you want to be a sales representative?"

He said, "Well, yes, but if it doesn't work, can I still be a customer service rep?"

I said, "Sure."

I referred him to a friend of mine in sales, fully expecting this guy to tell him, "Abandon hope." He referred him to his boss. His boss hired him.

About six months later, I ran into him one evening in a store and asked how he was doing.

"Oh, great," he said, "I've won this award, and that trophy, and this other thing, and . . . oh, it's after 7:00! Got to get home and get on the phone, you know!" He was a totally different guy!

A couple of years ago, I ran into him again, and learned he was earning well into six figures and loving life.

In another case, I met a potential client who had been a professional football player. I asked him what he wanted to do. He said, "I think I should be in middle management in a large corporation, learn the ropes, and work my way up." I had seen his resumé, and I knew that was the wrong answer, but didn't say anything about it at the time. He signed up as a client and we started meeting.

Each time we met, I would begin the meeting with, "What do you want to do?" Each time he would answer with the same, "I think I should be in middle management in a large corporation, learn the ropes, and work my way up." When I got this response consistently, I became more nervous, because I knew that was the wrong answer.

Finally, a week before we were to start the search, he came to see me, and I opened again with, "What do you want to do?"

He exploded! "I *hate* you!" and slammed his very large fist down on the desk hard enough to make it shake. "I don't want to *work* for a conglomerate! I want to *be* a conglomerate!"

"Okay," I said. "Let's go."

He became a conglomerate.

If you have no passion about what you have done, continuing to do it is a guarantee that you will be laid off in your next job. Go back and look at the examples of success you have written. Did you enjoy them? If not, identify examples that you did enjoy. I know it's not fun, but you'll thank me later. Do not put this assignment off. Not only is it some of the most important work you will do to prepare for your search, it is certainly the toughest.

# CHAPTER 3
# The Resumé & Profile

> *To get the right word in the right place*
> *is a rare achievement.*
> **– MARK TWAIN**

I n your job search, you will be using two types of documents. One you know as a resumé; the other is what I call a profile. They have very different purposes.

## Resumé

Everyone is in search of the perfect resumé, and everyone is an expert on other people's resumés. There isn't a soul in this country who won't gladly tell you exactly what is wrong with your resumé and what you must do to fix it. There is no job search expert more certain of himself than someone who has recently gotten a job. If you show it to two people, you can count on two opinions; frequently two diametrically opposed opinions. And those same two people have come to me at a job fair saying, "I know my resumé isn't the best . . .."

There is no such thing as a perfect resumé, but there is an unlimited number of bad ones.

A resumé is not a social, political, or religious statement. It is not a travelogue. It is not an objective, historical representation of your professional career. It is not a recitation of your experiences. It is not a legal document. Its purpose is not to summarize your skills and abilities, to tell the reader in capsule form who you are, or to assist the interviewer.

A resumé is an advertisement.

The purpose of a resumé is to get an interview. To understand how to structure one, you must first understand how employment works or, more accurately, how it doesn't work.

The rules most people learned about job hunting while they were growing up stipulate that they should send their resumé to Human Resources and wait for a phone call, but the odds that the phone will ring are not good. The HR rep's job is to get good people into the company—that's what they're paid for. But it isn't quite that simple.

Because of corporate downsizing, rightsizing, redeploying, outsourcing, and cost-cutting, the Human Resources representative is usually trying to do more work than is possible because the other people who did what he/she does are gone now. Moreover, an HR rep's understanding of the jobs they're trying to fill is typically inadequate, much more their understanding of what it takes to be good at these jobs. Moreover, every hiring manager that HR deals with thinks that their need is greater than all the others combined.

When I was a recruiter for a tech company, I was once cornered by the director of the satellite control center, who, standing in my doorway so I couldn't escape, said, "If you don't get me these people in the next couple of weeks, there will be no point in Intelsat launching the next generation of satellites, because we won't be able to *control* them!" Believe me, that will get your attention.

Say you're an antenna systems design engineer and the Human Resources representative needs to find one. If he or she doesn't already know who they're going to hire, it is likely that they will advertise. After all, the hiring manager has just spent the last twenty-five minutes explaining in no uncertain terms that if they don't find someone fast, the entire future of the organization is in doubt. Hence, the vacancy goes on the company's website.

How many applications do you think this will generate?

Back in the day, the HR rep would have placed an ad in the newspaper and response to it would have been limited by that newspaper's circulation. But now there is the internet. What's the limiting factor? There isn't one. Everyone on the planet with internet access can see the ad.

While HR might have gotten 300 responses to the ad before, they will get somewhere between 300 and 3,000 today.

Does the HR rep read these resumés at the office? In a small company where budgets are slim and they don't have resumé-reading software, one of two things will happen.

The HR rep will take years off their eyesight trying to read the resumés on the computer, or, not having time to read them at work, will print them out and take them home to read after dinner, after family talk about what everyone did that day, after getting the kids to bed, and so forth. Or maybe they'll log on from home and stare at the computer screen a while longer.

So, at 10:30 Tuesday night, under the lamp, with a headache, our HR rep is reading a hundred or more that came in that day. Yours is one of them. Here are some things to consider:

Is the HR rep trying to rule you in or out?

Out.

How much time do you think they're willing to devote to ruling you out?

Up to 10 seconds.

Do they understand the job they're trying to fill?

No.

Do they understand what you do for a living?

No.

It gets worse. How many people will they hire for this vacancy?

One.

How many resumés will they weed through?

Hundreds. Maybe thousands.

So, they are trying to hold hundreds or thousands of people out, while letting one in. But do they know which one? Do they even know that the right one will be in this batch of resumés?

No.

And will they get more resumés tomorrow?

Yes.

So, effectively, they are trying to keep everyone out.

Is this a logical process? No. Is it human? Very.

HR reps are tired and in a hurry, have a headache, don't understand the job, don't understand what you do, are trying to rule you out, and are willing to devote maybe ten seconds to do that. And if you're perfect for the vacancy but HR passes you up, will the hiring manager ever know? Will anyone know?

No. You won't either, because these days companies no longer respond to people who apply. You just sink silently into an ever-deepening black hole.

If the HR rep works for a company with a decent budget, they don't read all those resumés. They use software. HR reps don't even see the resumés that don't have the right keywords.

Again, is HR trying to rule you in or out?

Again, the answer is "Out."

Remember, this is only one job. They may have to fill several vacancies. And they may run an ad in the newspaper or call headhunters and get even more resumés.

Should you depend on HR to find you, the pearl, among all those swine? No.

This is just a glimpse of what happens when you send your resumé to a company so you'll understand how a resumé should be structured. Understand I'm not just some ne'er do well HR rep with a grudge to nurse. There were Human Resources people in every one of the fifty-one public workshops, presentations, or talks I gave in 2009 in which I talked about this process and, without exception, they agreed with me.

## The Resumé

The resumé, very simply, is a written advertisement for you. Therefore, anything on the resumé that facilitates getting an interview is good. Anything on the resumé that either doesn't facilitate getting an interview or that actively interferes with your getting an interview, is bad.

Let's take a look at the objective.

## The Objective

Many of those people who got a job, and therefore consider themselves experts on your resumé will advise you to have an objective on the resumé that pinpoints what it is you want to do to help the human resources rep know where to put you.

Balderdash!

Remember, the HR rep is trying to rule you out, not looking for a way to bring you in!

To help you get an interview, the objective will have to be so specific that it will rule out interviews for jobs similar to what you've targeted that you might otherwise be interested in, and for which you would qualify. To get around this obstacle by including similar jobs, the objective must be general to the point that it doesn't facilitate an interview.

Either way, the objective is bad.

Having read, or at least stared at, somewhere around a few hundred thousand resumés in my time, it seems to me that most begin with the objective, "A challenging position in a dynamic, growth-oriented company that rewards initiative . . .."

Goober's obvious goal here is to impress HR with the fact that he wants a challenge and recognizes theirs as a dynamic, growth-oriented company. He also doesn't have the remotest idea of what else to say, but his brother-in-law or the book he read said he had to have an objective, so he does. Besides, it must be good—he's seen it on so many other resumés!

This tactic can best be characterized as blatant sucking up. "A challenging position . . ." tells the reader absolutely nothing and is much like what those 99 other resumés' objectives in the stack read. Furthermore, the HR rep doesn't care what your objective is. They have their own objective. If Goober's objective doesn't match theirs, he's dead. He's just made it possible for the rep to rule him out, saving about five seconds.

So, if an objective is strategically unsound, what should you have at the top of your resumé? A summary of your background that presents you as the person you want to be seen to be (see the resumé format at the end of the chapter).

The second section of the resumé should be a reverse chronology, meaning the most recent first, of your employment, with a separate entry for each employer. Include one to three lines telling the reader what you did at each job. No more. If the job description is more than three lines, no one will read it. Never use the words, "Responsible for . . .." All sentences except for the summary start with action verbs.

Under each of these entries should be bulleted examples of success. These are critical. What you did at each job is experience. It does not sell you. It is there only to provide context for the reader. The achievement sells you. These will come from those examples of success you had to identify earlier. Use only the first and third sentences—did this, got this result. In deciding whether or not to see you, they don't care how you did it.

The last section is your education. The highest level of education is listed first, undergraduate last. If you don't have at least a bachelor's degree, don't bother with the education section unless your education specifically supports what you say you do, *e.g.*, training in technical schools.

Consider the fact that, in most cases, you'll either be emailing your resumé to someone or posting it on a website. Since many companies have software allowing them to do keyword searches, a little research is in order.

One of the things you need to find out is if you speak the language of the industry you want to remain in or enter. Do the research that will give you the keywords involved in the work that you're seeking, and make sure they are in your resumé.

### Passive Versus Active Writing Style

Consider writing style for a moment. Many in corporate America have learned to write in government-speak. This is a style in which everything is passive. One of the most succinct examples comes from the administration of President Clinton: "Mistakes were made."

This style of writing is preferred by the government because neither blame nor credit can be assigned. By saying, "Mistakes were made," one does not have to admit to having personally made a mistake as "I/We made a mistake" implies. By the same token, in saying "Efficiency was improved by 15 percent," no one stands out; therefore, neither personal blame nor personal success stands out. Goober doesn't want to stand out, because standing out is dangerous.

---

*If you're looking for a job, you'd better stand out!*

---

All statements in the resumé should be active—not passive. You will not say, "Costs were reduced by 10 percent." You will say, "Reduced costs by 10 percent," or, "Achieved a cost savings of 10 percent."

### Contact Information

This should include your name, address, phone number, and email address. Only.

Well, not quite. You will likely use your cell phone, as it is the only phone you have, but pay close attention to the next paragraph. Include your LinkedIn URL after making sure there is nothing there, or on any other social media, that can hurt you. Do not include your spouse's cell phone number, your personal web address, your Facebook, Twitter, or other social media, your address of record if it's different from your current address (unless you're moving there), or other similar types of information. Goober clutters up the heading with more contact information than anyone can use. Too much information is as bad as too little—it's distracting. There appears to be a trend today to not include the physical address (who's going to send you a letter anyway?). This is fine, but you should consider the hiring manager's or HR rep's mindset. If I don't see an address, my first thought is, "Am I going to have to relocate you?" My first action may be to throw it away.

### Cell Phone

Life being what it is, Goober is late for an interview, his seatbelt has put a permanent, unwanted crease in his suit, he's worrying about how to pay the bills, but if he can get through this yellow light, he just might make it to the interview on time, when some idiot cuts him off. He slams on the brakes and comes to a stop as the portfolio on the seat next to him slides off into the puddle of Coke the displaced can in the cup holder has created, staining both the portfolio and all copies of his resumé. He is five seconds into full-throated rage when his cell phone rings.

This is the call Goober has been hoping for. Quickly, he grabs the phone and answers it. Time out. Think he'll do a good job of handling it? I don't.

You put yourself at risk by allowing people unfettered access to you. Despite Goober's fear of being forgotten, if the company can't reach him the first time they try, they *will* leave a message or email him. If you're under 70 years old, your cell phone is probably your only phone, and this isn't a problem. Just remember, don't be like Goober. You don't have to answer it.

## Format
Regarding line justification, a fully justified document looks best. A ragged right edge is technically easier on the eye, and therefore easier to read, but the visual aspect of full justification will get you more points. It is better to spend the time adjusting word spacing than to lose points for appearance.

## Length
One page is fine; two pages are fine; three or more pages are totally unacceptable. One page has its advantages—if you've just graduated, you probably won't have more to talk about than that, the reader can get through it quickly, and two pages can become separated, but if you've done anything in your career, one page may be logistically difficult. Two pages are perfectly fine. There may have been a time when resumés were only one page, but that was when people didn't go to college or have more than one job for their entire career. A three-page resumé is fatal. Resumés that appear only online can be more, because the software doesn't care that you're breaking the rules.

Goober calls his resumé a Curriculum Vitae, because to him that sounds more distinguished. To be sure, if you are in academia, this is the term to use. But the document is not at all interchangeable with the resumé. *Curricula vitae* are evaluated by the pound, so don't worry about the number of pages—the more, the better.

## Paper

You're thinking, "Paper. Seriously? You're talking about paper? I haven't used paper in quite a while," and starting to ask yourself just how old this guy Whitehouse is. Bear with me for a minute. I know that resumés hardly ever touch paper any more. I'm not at all saying that you should use paper, but there may come a time, like when you show up for an interview, or when you actually have to mail your resumé, when you will have to use paper. If so, you need to know what to use. And it's all about human nature, not style.

In the event your resumé must touch paper, it should be printed on 24#, linen finish, off-white, watermarked paper. Do not use gray, or any other color. Gray as corporate stationery looks good, but at 10:30 Tuesday night, under the lamp, with a headache, gray is depressing. Depress the HR rep and you don't get an interview. Never use white, even high quality white—95 percent of all resumés are printed on plain white copier paper, so it will get lost in the stack with those. Goober wants his resumé to stand out, so he prints it on bright yellow paper. But, unless you are a graphic artist, in which case your resumé must be totally unique, the use of colors shows the reader that you don't know the rules.

The paper should be watermarked (typically the manufacturer's logo embedded in the paper). A watermark says quality. No watermark says cheap. When you print, make darn sure the watermark is right side up and frontward. There are people out there whose first act of reading a resumé is to hold it up to the light. If there is no watermark, or it is upside down or backwards, their second act is to throw it away unread. This may seem especially anal to you, and I can make an argument that you're right, but Rule #1 in the candidate selection process is, "When you're trying to rule people out, any excuse will do." I had a client who found herself in the hiring mode. She called me one morning, saying, "I was thinking about you at ten o'clock last night. I was going through a stack of resumés, I looked down and saw that the next one was on pink paper, and my first thought was, 'At least I don't have to read *that* one!'"

Use this type of paper if you print your resumé—any time you print your resumé (except one, which I'll talk about later). Don't get lazy. I often attend job fairs (another place you actually need a resumé on paper) and offer a free resumé review and am shocked at the number of people who show up with resumés printed on copier paper. I tell these people, "You can't do that." What amazes me is the response I most often get: "Yes, I know. I just did this for the job fair." So, Goober, you came to the job fair to *not* impress people? Presumably they see the job fair as an opportunity to talk with and impress a real person who represents a company, an opportunity that is rare, indeed. And they think that copier paper will impress? More importantly, do they think it will stand out later in the stack of 200 other resumés printed on copier paper that the company representative takes home?

## Human Nature

Here's why all the fuss about paper. Everyone who picks up a resumé feels it. They rub the paper between their thumb and forefinger, and if they feel texture, they feel good. Human nature strikes again. The paper's finish is important.

There are a couple of types of paper finishes. Those you see most often are laid and linen. While I really prefer laid, because a laid finish has more texture, it does not hold toner well, even the laid finish made especially for laser printers, so I recommend linen. You must have a pretty good sense of touch to feel a linen finish, but it's there. You can also see it, so it isn't just smooth, like the copier paper most people use.

There is a complication to what I've been saying. If the HR rep or hiring manager is a millennial, they are totally familiar with 20# white copier paper and seem to view the paper I'm talking about as a foreign concept. If you hand them a resumé printed on 24# off-white, linen finish, watermarked paper, they may look at you funny and think, "How old-school!" But they'll still feel the paper!

I advocate using a laser printer to print. Ink has gotten much better over the years, but it still isn't great. Many people favor customizing the resumé for the individual company or person. I don't.

One last thing about packaging. At job fairs, I sometimes see Goober handing out resumés in special envelopes or folders as though they were gold certificates. This practice labels him as someone living in the late 19th century and will cause his resumé to be placed in the first available trash can.

## More Than One Resumé?

Several years ago, when I was an HR rep for a Fortune 500 company, I received a call one night from an engineer who wanted to know if his resumé had arrived. I had no idea, as my secretary had logged over 400 that day. For some reason, we struck up a conversation, and in that conversation, he let it slip that he had seven different resumés and couldn't remember which one he had sent me. His was one of very few names I have written down with the express purpose of keeping them out. Why? He was telling me that he would be whoever I wanted him to be. I don't hire people like that. I hire people who know who they are and are looking for an opportunity to *be* who they are.

By creating multiple resumés for yourself, you're like the guy above—virtually saying you don't know who you want to be. You create a logistical nightmare for yourself in terms of tracking what you sent to whom. The easiest way to get ruled out is to say, "Oh, I guess I sent you the wrong resumé—let me get you the right one."

You should be able to present yourself in one resumé. If you need to accentuate certain things for a certain company, do it in the cover letter.

## Cover Letter

When it comes to cover letters, one size does not fit all. I tremble when so-called experts treat the cover letter as if you could possibly say the same thing to everyone and make sense to anyone. Every cover letter needs to be individually written. There are styles that are similar, but every letter should be written specifically for the person reading it.

## Internet

Email has become a standard way of transmitting resumés, much more standard than the U.S. Postal Service. While you can transmit your resumé as a Word (or other word-processing software) file, I recommend saving your resumé as a PDF file and transmitting it that way. Why? I'm paranoid. It takes more effort to change a PDF than a Word document. If the company requires a Word document, protect it with a password. Yes, I am paranoid. But paranoia doesn't mean they're not out to get you.

Save your resumé as a text file if you plan on pasting it on companies' websites. This is a bit of a pain because saving the document as a text file wreaks havoc with the formatting. Once you have saved it, close it; then go back in and fix the formatting. Yours will look 90 percent better than all the others.

## The Profile

Never confuse the profile with the resumé. (See the profile format at the end of the chapter.) They have totally different purposes. The purpose of the resumé is to get an interview. That's the only thing it's good for. The purpose of the profile is for use in the referral process I'll be discussing later. Only Goober would use it as a resumé, and he would get very few interviews with it.

Back in my headhunting days, I quickly recognized a certain style of resumé. It had an objective, a list of achievements, an employment history, and an education section. But you couldn't tell where or when the achievements were made. It was frustrating. Everyone I knew in the search business hated the style.

One day I discovered that someone out there was teaching this to people, and I made it a life goal to hunt them down and kill them, because they were ruining people's careers.

Fast-forward more than fifteen years. I had just obtained employment with a national career advising firm that taught people how to get a job and coached them through the search. On my first day on the job, I opened the client manual, turned to the resumé section, and immediately discovered who it was who was teaching people to prepare the resumé I so hated.

This is terrible, I thought. I'll have to resign. I can't be a party to this!

But the fact was, I couldn't afford to resign. I needed the money. This caused me to give considerable thought to the style of the document. After about a week, I understood what was going on.

In the 1940s, the firm's founder invented everything associated with today's outplacement industry. He called the document a marketing brochure. (This may have been fine in the 1940s, but don't do it today.) Why would he do that? I believe he wanted to distinguish it from a resumé. He never intended it to be a resumé. But over the years, people lost sight of the original intent and used it as a resumé.

So why would you want to put together a document such as this?

Just as the resumé has a specific purpose—to get you an interview, the profile has one—to create questions in the mind of the reader.

You may have heard the profile referred to as a functional resumé. It isn't. The true functional resumé typically doesn't include a specific employment history. This is the functional resumé's chief drawback—it's easy to hide time spent in prisons with the true functional resumé, so its credibility with almost everyone is low to nonexistent, mostly nonexistent.

Again, its purpose is to create questions in the mind of the reader. Why would you want to do that? Because you will be sitting across from the reader and be able to answer those questions. In the ensuing conversation, you start looking smart.

The profile will have an objective, followed by achievements, followed by employment history, followed by education. There is something in the human psyche that wants to match achievement to employment. Not facilitating this causes confusion. If it's 10:30 Tuesday night, after sifting through dozens of resumés, the HR rep is tired and irritable. If the profile is confusing, he also gets angry. Is this a good format to use for a resumé? Goober would, but you won't.

Start with an objective. The person sitting across the desk wants to know what you are trying to accomplish. The objective can always be changed based upon what you learn in the referral process. It should typically be brief: a specific job name or type of work. Remember, the point of this document isn't to get an interview—you're already sitting in front of someone. The purpose here is to see if that person concurs with your objective, what he or she calls the kind of job you're looking for, and whether you are the kind of person who would be of value to the organization.

Next, simply list the achievements that best support your objective in a section called Achievements between the objective and the employment history. The achievements should be stripped of any information that would tell the reader where you were, or how you accomplished the achievement. Once again, use only the first and third sentences for each achievement. This is critical. The whole point of the profile is to frustrate and create questions in the mind of the person facing you. "You did that? How did you do it? Where were you when you did it? Tell me more about this!"

In this conversation you start to look pretty darned smart. You're a hero!

## Communication

This brings up another point—jargon. And it applies to both the resumé and the profile. The military, as well as many industries and professions have their own jargon. You cannot assume that the jargon from your field will transfer, especially if you're leaving the military. Communication is effective only if the guy behind the desk understands what you're talking about.

This is important in learning the language of whatever industry to which you are headed. Likewise, you must give up the language of your previous existence, unless you are going to remain within that environment, in which case you absolutely must keep it.

## Style

A word about the resumé's or the profile's appearance. When I was in the search business and, subsequently in corporate HR, there was a guy in the area who worked with transitioning military. He gave his clients a resumé format to follow and a writing style to use. Presumably because the military wasn't in high regard at the time, he told his clients to hide the fact that they were military. Unfortunately, that was impossible. When I first recognized that the writer was covering up that fact, I wondered what else he might be hiding and threw the resumé away. Later, when I had seen enough of these resumés to be able to recognize the style immediately, I didn't even have to read them before I threw them away.

The point is, while I am giving you a format to use, I strongly advise you to use your own choices for the header, font style, etc., so your resumé doesn't look the same as everyone else's, causing some cynic like me to recognize the style and immediately question the validity of the whole thing.

## Summary

You will be using two different documents with specifically different purposes—the resumé and the profile.

The resumé is simply an ad for you. Its sole purpose is to get an interview. It does this by presenting you as a successful person, not once, but repeatedly. It has a summary of no more than four lines of text that present you as the person you want to be seen to be, all in objective, not subjective terms. This is followed by a reverse chronology of your work history, including employer's name, dates of employment, your title, no more than three lines explain duties and responsibilities, followed by bullets showing success. This is followed by an education segment.

The purpose of the profile is to create questions, not to get an interview. It leads off with an objective that describes the kind of work you're looking for, an achievement section that shows success without naming employers or telling how the success was achieved. This is followed by an employment section (reverse chronology), and an education section.

You have an option to take the profile to an interview the resumé got you, but you must be cautious with its use. Forcing it on the interviewer may bring dire consequences. Confusing that person is the last thing you want to do, and he or she probably doesn't have the foggiest idea of what a profile is, or why you are giving it to them.

## Resumé Format

**NAME**
**Address**
**Email Address**
**Phone Number**

**SUMMARY**
Three to four lines positioning you as the person you want to be seen to be.

**EXPERIENCE**
COMPANY NAME, City, State            year-present
Title
Description of work performed, management role, etc.; no more than three lines. All sentences start with action verbs.
- Success
- Success
- Success

COMPANY NAME, City, State            year-present
Title
Description of work performed, management role, etc.; no more than three lines. All sentences start with action verbs.
- Success
- Success
- Success

COMPANY NAME, City, State                    year-present
Title
Description of work performed, management role, etc.; no more than three lines. All sentences start with action verbs.
- Success
- Success
- Success

**EDUCATION**
NAME OF COLLEGE/UNIVERSITY, City, State
Degree; Concentration

**NOTE:** Fonts:  either Arial 11 point for text, 12 point for headings, or Times New Roman 12 point for text, 13 point for headings;
I use this format because it's logical and easy to read. It isn't a requirement.

# Profile Format

**NAME**
**Address**
**Email Address**
**Phone Number**

### OBJECTIVE
*One to three lines of text naming the job or type of work you want to do, as well as the environment/ industry.*
*Example:* A position involving the improvement of sales through the development or enhancement of catalog sales programs.

### SUMMARY
*Two to four (no more) lines of text—no bullets— describing you as the person you want to be seen to be.*
*Example:* Fourteen years of business development, systems analysis, strategic planning, and marketing initiatives in the financial services, automotive, nonprofit, and retail industries. Specific expertise in improving business processes. Documented record of getting to the root of the problem and developing viable, cost effective solutions which improve productivity and profitability.

### ACHIEVEMENTS
Eight to 12 bulleted achievements that best support your objective. If the profile is one page, the two most important go first, the third most important last, and

the others ranked in order following the second most important. Example: 1,2,4,5,6,7,8.9,3

If the profile goes to two pages (perfectly acceptable) the two most important achievements go first, the third at the bottom of page one, the fourth at the top of page two, and those that don't fit on page one, following the fourth on page two. Example: Page 1: 1,2,5,6,7,8,9,3; Page 2:4,10,11

The reason for this structure is that when the human eye is confronted with a page of bullets it gets confused. As a result, people will read the first bullet because it's first. They'll read the second faster, and then race to the bottom of the page and read the last, and the first on the second page. Those positions are where you want the most important achievements.

**EMPLOYMENT**
COMPANY NAME, City, State                    year-present
Title
No more than three lines regarding what you did. All selling is done in the achievements.

**EDUCATION**
FAMOUS UNIVERSITY, CITY, State
Degree; Concentration/major

**NOTE**: Fonts:  either Arial 11 point for text, 12 point for headings, or Times New Roman 12 point for text, 13 point for headings;
I use this format because it's logical and easy to read. It isn't a requirement.

# CHAPTER 4

# The Sound Bite

> *Be sincere; be brief; be seated.*
> — FRANKLIN D. ROOSEVELT

It is essential that you have a statement ready that describes you, your background, and your capabilities without causing the interviewer to nod off into a well-earned nap or quickly change the topic to the weather. Rather, it should generate interest in you and what you do.

I call this statement the sound bite. You are probably familiar with its concept. It is a brief statement designed to create an image that encapsulates a subject.

Why use it here?

## "Tell Me About Yourself."

This is the most common opening to an interview. When you ace this question, the interviewer will sit up and start listening.

The answer to "Tell me about yourself" is the sound bite, and this is its only purpose. Its goal is to give the interviewer an answer to the question relevant to your reason for sitting here. It is also the most critical point in the interview—it's the opening shot in your taking over. More about that later.

The sound bite has three parts.

---

*Part 1: "I have X years' experience in Y." X is the number of years you're selling, and Y is a word or phrase that tells how you spent those years.*

---

My sound bite begins, *"I have over twenty years of experience in what I would call the employment marketplace."*

I'm selling over twenty years. I have over thirty years of experience, but if I say thirty years to a 25-year old, they will assume I'm too old to have any relevance for them.

Be a little careful about this since you must also cover the time.

I once had a client who came in after he had developed the sound bite, and I said, "Tell me about yourself." He said, "Well, I've got twelve years' experience in manufacturing." He went on to tell me about this experience, which was fine, except that he was 60 years old and looked it. My first reaction as the hiring manager was, "So where'd you spend the other twenty-five years—prison?"

You must cover the time.

---

*Part 2: "I have been these things, and I have done those*

*things." These things are generic titles; those things are functions of the work you've done.*

---

I'll go on to say, *"I've been a search consultant or headhunter, a corporate recruiter, a human resources manager, an organization development consultant, and a corporate outplacement consultant. I've placed accountants and telecommunications people, hired spacecraft designers and earth station managers. In outplacement, I've worked with CEOs, college professors . . . and the occasional felon."*

---

*Part 3: "I am most effective at A, B, and C." A, B, and C can be special skills, they can be functions of the work you've done, or want to do, they can be a combination of the two.*

---

You know you can't say, "I'm good." Your mom taught you that, and she was right. Goober knows that too, so he falls back on, "I enjoy doing this and that and the other," hoping the hiring manager will make the mental leap from "enjoy" to "do well." Frankly, he couldn't care less what Goober enjoys. In the unlikely event that he hires him, and they become friends, some day he might care what Goober enjoys, but today, he's trying to kill him. So that's fatal. But if you say, "I'm most effective . . .," people believe it.

*"I'm probably most effective at helping people find better careers, coaching them through the search process, and motivating them to do things they might have trouble doing on their own."*

Helping people find better careers is a function of what I do. Coaching and motivating are developed skills that I have.

Let's go back to part two. I said I'd hired spacecraft designers and earth station managers, and that may or may not have made an impact on the hiring manager. I went on to say that in outplacement, I'd worked with CEOs, college professors, and the occasional felon. That probably got a bigger reaction.

I do this intentionally. The sound bite is essentially a monologue. It comes at the beginning of the interview and sets the tone for the interview. If I lose the interviewer during the sound bite, I'm dead—I've lost him forever. Spacecraft designers, earth station managers, and felons are hooks. They're there to keep the interviewer with me.

If his attention is starting to wander, the odds are that spacecraft designers or earth station managers will get him back. The same goes for felon. If he's starting to think about what he might have for dinner tonight, felon snaps him back into the conversation very quickly. It's totally unexpected in the context of what I'm saying.

You need to have a sound bite that describes you to the hiring manager or the interviewer. Make sure it has a hook or two in it—preferably in Part 2, because, if they're inclined to take a nap during the interview, their eyelids will start to get heavy during your recitation of your work history.

The sound bite can be no less than forty seconds long. If it's 39.8 seconds, the interviewer won't care what you've said; it wasn't enough.

Goober's response to "Tell me about yourself," is, "What would you like to know?" This is lethal. It puts Goober totally at the mercy of the interviewer, who says, "I'd like to know your mortgage interest divided by your shoe size." How well do you think Goober will handle that one?

It cannot be a tenth of a second longer than 75 seconds—a minute and a quarter. If it's a minute and 16 seconds long, you *have* exceeded the hiring manager's attention span, he *is* thinking about what he'll have for dinner, and you're dead. Forty-five to 60 seconds is the ideal length.

Last, and this may sound silly, it must be casual English. Bear with me. Here's what Goober will do. He'll sit down with a piece of paper and a pencil, or keyboard, and start composing. He'll edit it, polish it, make it great, memorize it, and feed it back when asked, "Tell me about yourself," and the interview will be over, because the interviewer can recognize *canned* when he hears it.

The spoken word and the written word are dramatically different. Written English is long sentences with commas and phrases and big words like "therefore." Casual English is short sentences with "uhs" and "ums" and small words, like "so."

This doesn't mean that you shouldn't write it out. Most people probably should, as that's how most of us keep track of our thoughts. But, once you have it written out, you must translate it into casual conversational English, and then you have to think of as many different ways of saying it as you can.

I've done the Bud Whitehouse sound bite in three parts here. There isn't one of those parts that I can't replace at least four times. This is important, because when you're sitting there in the interview, working from lists of words in your head, selecting the words to use for the other person, it appears to the other person that the whole thing is extemporaneous—you're thinking it up as you go.

Once you've developed the sound bite, learn it so well that it isn't memorized; it's known—it's part of you. Practice it in all its forms so many times that you can say it perfectly, with just the right inflection, just the right conversational tone, just the right panache, that the listener is dutifully impressed, while you're thinking about what you need to pick up at the grocery store on the way home.

A good way to learn it that well is to go to your spouse or significant other and say, "From this moment on, until I am employed, you have the right to ask me at any time of the day or night, regardless of what's going on, 'Tell me about yourself.' I have to respond, and I can't do it the same way twice in a row."

You'll have it down in about two days!

# CHAPTER 5

# The Search Plan

> *In preparing for battle I have always found that*
> *plans are useless, but planning is indispensable.*
> **– DWIGHT D. EISENHOWER**

S o, where are we in terms of preparation? We've discussed how reality differs from what you may have learned from the American job culture. We've talked about what you can offer an employer and how to sell it in a way the employer can understand and appreciate and profiles, their intended uses, and effective ways of framing them. Next up, we'll plan the search. This is one of the critical stages in the process. I've given up asking potential clients what their plan for the search is. Spending six hours a day on line is *not* a plan. But the search plan provides the structure necessary for a proactive search. If your search isn't proactive, you are essentially sitting around, waiting for something to happen to you. This is rarely productive.

Before we do that, though, let me point out a way that some can avoid the job search altogether. That would be to buy a job. Buying a business could be a good way of creating employment, especially if you are retiring from the military or a company, as opposed to being separated from it. Many who are retiring tend to have more in the way of available assets to invest in a business. You could start a business, buy an existing business, or buy a franchise.

If you are seriously interested in acquiring a business, franchises are a good thing to consider. The failure rate of small business startups is staggering, but about 90 percent of franchises are successful, and many cost less than a profitable non-franchise business. If the idea is appealing, find yourself an expert in franchise acquisition. One of the best ways of losing all your money is to go into it alone, and that is totally unnecessary when there are people who specialize in qualifying and helping others navigate that maze.

But if you are not interested in that, or cannot afford to consider business acquisition as a realistic alternative, read on. Prepare for the search first by focusing on location. It isn't uncommon for a client to tell me, "I'd move just about anywhere for the right job." But this only works if jobs are coming at him from everywhere, and the challenge is to select the best one from among many. The problem with this line of thought is that you can't look everywhere productively. The search zone needs to be pretty narrow—like a city. This may seem counterintuitive, but it is faster to work one city at a time than it is to try to look everywhere at once.

Enough about where to look. Let's look at how to look. I'll come back to this point later.

There are lots of ways of getting a job. The methods most often referred to are "networking," which we've been discussing, ads (almost always the internet) and headhunters.

Let's talk numbers for a minute. Remember, back at the beginning of the book, I explained that many jobs were never vacancies, that by looking for vacancies Goober was giving up as much as two thirds of the market, and that that big percentage is what people know as the hidden job market. Well, it's hiding in plain sight, and that's why we structure the search process around looking for a person with a problem.

Remember when I said that you've probably heard this process referred to most often as networking? Let's take a moment to talk about words.

Unfortunately, over the years events have tarnished terms involved in the job hunting process. Words don't mean today what they did years ago. Networking used to mean that you're acquiring a group (network) of like-minded people who will help you become more visible in the marketplace, and you will also help them. But, because of the Goobers of the world, the word has been corrupted, and now when it is used, what people hear is that they are being asked to sponsor someone for a job. They react by heading for the exits.

Another misguided term is information interview, coined, I believe, in the 1970s, and again so badly abused that baby boomers who were around then will hang up on you if you use it. Strictly speaking, the term means sitting with someone who has knowledge or experience in a particular type of work and getting the information you need to know if you would enjoy it and be qualified for it. Over not many years, it devolved to mean getting access to a hiring manager under the guise of seeking information and, while there, bludgeoning them into hiring you. That's bad enough but consider the word interview. Both hiring managers and job hunters are scared by the word, so why use it?

I prefer to use the term referral process because (a) I have to call it something, and (b) it hasn't been abused yet and it's accurate. As the guy who hired me years ago said, "You move from trust to trust." But I would not use the term with someone you're meeting. It would distract and disrupt the conversation flow. You'll also find that I often use the term networking because sometimes, although dangerous, it's easier to use terms people are familiar with, and I'm lazy.

Now we're going to put together a search plan. In doing so, we want to keep the odds in mind, while not forgetting alternatives. A good job search consists of working all the options, while focusing on those most likely to pay off.

We are going to start the search plan by looking at who you know.

To make it easier to think, here are some categories for consideration.

- Friends and acquaintances—yours and your significant other's
- References, both business and personal
- "Force multipliers," *i.e.,* people who know a lot of people, *e.g.,* bankers, attorneys, accountants, insurance representatives, financial planners, stock brokers, real estate agents, mortgage brokers, doctors, dentists, government officials, politicians, mechanics, hairdressers/beauticians, clergy, etc.
- Former employers (superiors, peers, subordinates)/ competitors
- Group affiliations (churches, fitness clubs, racquet clubs, golf clubs, country clubs, networking groups, youth soccer, Little League, Boy Scouts, Girl Scouts, Moose

Club, Lions Club, Elks Club, Rotary Clubs, bowling leagues, fishing/hunting clubs, fraternities/sororities, etc.)
- Vendors
- Clients
- Alumni
- Professional/Trade associations

Sit down with your spouse/significant other/friend/ roommate and go through each category, figuring out just how many people you know in each one. Write as many names as you can think of. *Do not filter the list!* Write down everyone, no matter who or where they are.

For example, the first category is friends and acquaintances. You know what a friend is. Acquaintances are a sleeper category. The folks like the soccer mom, the scoutmaster, *et cetera*, who may not come to mind at first, but can be really useful in a job search. This category alone should result in dozens, perhaps hundreds of names.

Next is references. How many people do you know who could tell a prospective employer what a great employee you would make? Obviously, these might people to whom you have reported in the past. Only use peers if necessary. A prospective employer can relate to your boss a whole lot easier than to your peer. Next are personal references. Who do you know who could tell a prospective employer what a great person you are? These cannot be the same people who just told the employer what a great employee you would be.

Continue through the list, writing down the names of everyone you know. But now we have a problem. I'm providing categories for you to consider because it will help you think. Human nature dictates that if I ask you who you know at Bank of America, Verizon, or Capital One, you can tell me in a heartbeat. But if I just ask you who you know, you have no idea where to start and your brain will shut down. I'm helping you think. But human nature *also* dictates that you will naturally confine yourself to the categories I'm providing. Don't do that. Be creative. Come up with your own categories to add to these.

Give this process a total effort for 45 to 60 minutes. Then put aside. By doing this you will have started a thought process somewhere in your brain that will continue to work in background, producing names at odd hours of the day and night. Write them down—they're good ones

---

*Warning: It is easy to rule people out! "Oh, yeah—Ralph. But I haven't seen Ralph in two years. He probably can't help anyway!" The fact is you have no idea whether Ralph can help. You might be amazed at who knows whom in this undertaking. The world is a very small place. Do not edit the list by assuming someone you've thought of can't or won't help.*

*People (especially introverts) do this kind of thing frequently. They tell themselves that contacting Ralph won't help, when it's the thought of contacting Ralph that makes them uncomfortable, so if they can rule Ralph out, then they don't have to contact him. If Ralph can't or won't help, let him tell you. Don't make the decision for him!*

---

You should be able to come up with at least twelve names in each category. If you can't think of twelve, keep thinking. You know *many* more people than you realize at first. The idea here is to stretch your brain a little. According to the experts, you know somewhere around 2,000 people.

It used to be said that you are eight people away from knowing everyone in the world. A few years ago, scientists calculated the number to 6.27. Recently, probably due to the popularity of social media, the number dropped to 3.57. So, in theory at least, you are less than four people away from a person with a problem. This corresponds to my own experience. Once you reach the third person in a networking chain, you should be talking with someone who can hire you. If this isn't the case, something is wrong.

I once worked with a Marine with thirty years of service. He started military life as a private, worked all the way to the top of the enlisted ranks, started over at the bottom of the officer ranks, and finished his military career as a full colonel. He sat in front of me and swore he didn't know a soul. For a half hour, we went back and forth, until finally I said, "You're not leaving here until I get a name."

Within 10 seconds he said, "Oh, yeah. My ex-brother-in-law is CEO of a Fortune 500 company." His ex-brother-in-law referred him to the person who hired him.

You will be using this plan in the job search, but remember Eisenhower's words. Make a plan, but don't tie yourself to it. As much as we talk about being proactive, you must be able to react to circumstances that will arise outside of your plan.

This is likely to be a true growth process for you. In doing this you will improve your ability to talk with people you don't know, to think quickly and adroitly, to see yourself as the solution to a problem, and not a job hunter, you will develop relationships that may last a lifetime, and you will build a lasting network that will provide future employment for as long as you manage it well.

Remember the lady from the front of the book who was certain she would get a job but would miss talking to all those wonderful people? She was not enthusiastic about this when she started. Neither was I, when I last looked for a job. I'm strongly introverted, didn't like talking to people I didn't know, and didn't like having to go see them. But the resulting meetings were some of the most fun I've had relative to work, and the fellow who hired me still sends me White House Christmas ornaments every year!

If you're willing to risk talking to people you don't know, you can gain much more than your own growth. The truth is you wind up talking to people who have the same interests you do, you have great conversations, and each one hands you on to the next until one of them hires you.

Most people look at this in terms of acquiring a new skill. In seminars, I used to draw a big triangle on the whiteboard, divide it into four levels, and label the top level Excellent. "Everyone wants to be excellent at what they do," I would say, to the general acknowledgement of the participants. In the level below excellent, I would write Good. "Before you can be excellent, you must first be good." More nodding of heads. In the third level down, I would write Bad, and say, "Before you can be good you first have to be bad," to general laughter. Writing on the lowest level, I would turn to the group and say, "To achieve bad, you must first Try."

I had a client who disappeared for weeks after the seminar. Finally, he scheduled an appointment and came to see me. I was ready to kill him for disappearing. Walking back to my office I said, "Where have you been?"

He said, "Oh, I was out getting bad." *Good answer.* I had to honor that.

Now back to the plan. If you are unemployed, your goal is eight to ten referral meetings per week. Most people can handle that without too much trouble.

The key to success is to hit the search as hard as possible in the first week. Assuming you have at least twelve friends and twelve business and personal references, call all twenty-four people in the first week and schedule as many meetings as you can. This is a very easy process to slow down; it is very difficult to speed it up, because you're always at the mercy of other people's schedules.

To find a good job, you need two things: a list of targets, and a list of people who can get you into them. If you can only have one, have a list of targets. You can find people anywhere.

Before going to talk to people, make a list. A target is not necessarily a company to which you want to devote your life. It is a company in which you have at least a tentative interest. Perhaps you can make a list without having to do research. If not, go to your local library, create a username and get information on how to use *Reference USA*, an online database with information on a staggering number of companies, available for free through many library systems. Your goal here is to make a list of eight to twelve companies you would like to find out more about. You will show this list to everyone you talk with. "I have a tentative interest in these companies," you will say. "Who would you know in these companies? Who would you know who *would* know people in these companies? What companies might be like these that I should consider? Who would you know in those companies? Who would you know who *would* know people in those companies?" This is how you will gain access to those targets.

Start with your friends. Call your friend and say, "I'm going to be starting up a job search. (If your friend already knows you're searching say, "I've pushed the reset button on the job search.") I've taken some time out, done some thinking, and put together a new profile. I think I'm about ready to get started. Before I do though, I'd like to sit down with you for about a half hour and get a little advice, a little feedback. When can we meet?"

Schedule a meeting. Go see them. Show them the profile and the target list. "This is who I am now. This is what I'm trying to accomplish. Do you think I can do it?" Most will agree. If they don't, the meeting is over. If they do, you say, "Great! Thought so myself. Here's my problem. I can tell you more about what I've done, where I've done it, and who I've done it with, than you would ever want to know. What I can't tell you is what's going on in the business community now, because I've had my head down doing my job (or I'm new here, or . . .). I need to find out what's going on—who's here, who's doing well, who's not, who has opportunities, who has challenges, etc. And I need to get as much of that kind of information as I can before I go running around trying to get people to hire me." Refer them to the target list. "Put yourself in my place for a moment. If you were looking for that kind of information, who would you go to?"

And I'll tell you who I would go to, because I don't have to go out of my way, or make a commitment to do something, or take a risk—the three deadly sins of job hunting.

You will say, "Great! Just what I was looking for. Would you mind if I contact them and use your name in referral?" And I'll say, "No problem."

Call your references, and if they have already agreed to be references, say, "In a moment of weakness, you agreed to be a reference for me. I just want you to know I'm holding you to it! What I'd really like is for you to be an *informed* reference. I've taken some time out, done some thinking, put together a new profile. I'd like to get together with you, go over the profile, explain what I'm trying to accomplish, so that when your phone *does* ring, you'll have a better idea of what's going on."

Schedule a meeting. Go see them. That meeting is the same as the meeting with your friend.

Distance becomes an issue here. You will find that getting someone's complete attention requires you to sit in front of them. That said, it's a big country. I would suggest that a two hour drive time is reasonable to get in front of someone (but I live on the dense east coast). Beyond that, it's probably going to be a phone call, unless you can get them to use Skype or zoom, or some similar online meeting app. Recognize, though, that productivity may degrade with distance.

How to solve this? Remember when I said at the beginning that it is more effective to search one geographic location at a time, rather than many all at once? I had a client who lived in Charlottesville, Virginia, who first targeted Seattle for the search. He knew one person there. He went to Seattle for five days, having scheduled that person for day one. He came back east a week later, saying, "Seattle isn't a target anymore. They're not doing what I want to do." Next, he targeted Minneapolis. On his return, having spent a week there, he opened his front door to a ringing phone, with a job offer from his target company in Minneapolis.

So, where do you want to meet? I would strongly urge you to meet people in their workplace if possible. I'm not thinking business when I'm sitting by the grill with a beer. And I'm on down time if we go to lunch during the week. You want me thinking business. Where do I do that? In my office!

Say we meet. I'd like to help you. I give you one name. Your response is, "Great! I'll be contacting this person over the next couple of days. If you were me, would you write to them first, and follow up with a phone call? Or would you send them an email? Or would you just call them up? Then take my advice—I know the person you'll be trying to reach. I had a client who was 20-something and the web master for a large intranet website. I said to her, "Now, you'd probably prefer to get an email," and she said, "Oh, please! I get 200 emails a day! A letter's special!"

Now here is a potential problem. If you are an introvert, you would probably rather lick sand than talk to people you don't know. It may be tempting to use letters as a delaying tactic. Goober would convince himself that he's actively seeking employment by writing the letters, but he can relax a little because it will be two or three days until he follows up. But you recognize the fact that you're not Goober, you're on a mission, and that waiting days before doing anything isn't part of the mission. You are unstoppable!

If I give you two names, your response is, "Oh, fantastic! If you were me, which one would you contact first? Okay, over the next few days I'll contact these people in this order. If you were me, would you write to them first, etc.?"

If I give you three or more names, your response is, "This is unbelievable! Fantastic! If you were me, who would you contact first? Who would you contact second? Who would you contact . . .?" Make me prioritize the list up to five. If the next few days are wide open, "Okay. Over the next few days I'll contact these first five people in this order. I'll get back to you before I try to reach the others. Would you write to them . . .?" If over the next week, you are up to your eyebrows in stuff, "Okay. It's probably going to be about a week before I can contact any of these people. When I do, I'll start with the first three. I'll contact them in this order. I'll get back to you before I contact any of the others. Would you write to them . . .?" This is how you control the flow of the search. It's also how you stay alive.

Is this manipulation? Is it badgering? No. Showing the questions this way might lead you to think so, but remember, you're only reading one half of the conversation, and the person doing the referring isn't going to refer you to one, two, three, four, *and* five people. They will refer you to only one of those.

Why do it this way?

Goober and I meet during the week and I give him five names. By 5 pm Friday, he's reached the first three of these people. At 9 am Saturday, I'm playing tennis with person number five. We play a set, we're standing by the water cooler catching our breath, and I remember! "Say, did you get a call this week from Goober Smokebreak?" I ask. "*Who?*" he responds. And Goober's dead to me. It won't occur to me that he and I met only a couple of days ago. It will occur to me that he asked for my help and I gave it willingly. And he's wasted it, worm that he is!

The point is that you don't want people who are helping you, and who may become permanent members of your network, to get nasty surprises. You need to keep them in the loop. When you schedule meetings with people they have referred you to, get back to them and tell them. When your meetings with people they refer you to bear fruit, get back to them and tell them. When you are unable to get through to people they refer you to, get back to them and ask for assistance. This, again, is all about developing and maintaining relationships.

A note about tracking. You want to keep thorough, up-to-date records concerning who you have met with, the outcome and/or referrals gained, etc. Once you have a new job, you will be going through this record to determine who joins your network and who does not. Most of my clients have found, short of investing in relationship management software, that an Excel spreadsheet is the most effective tool.

While we're at it, let's talk a moment about the use of social media in the search.

## Social Media

Your primary tools here are (as of this writing) Facebook and LinkedIn. Here is the *caveat*: while social media can be useful in a search, you must never depend on them to get you a job. Just as technology has made hiring easier, but not more effective, for the employer, it has made it easier, but not more effective, for you to reach out to people. To succeed, you are going to have to sit before several, perhaps many people. Social media channels are primarily *research* tools to find people to sit in front of.

Speaking of research, Indeed (indeed.com) is a useful tool to learn or better understand the language of an industry you're interested in. It, and other industry advertising, will give you the words you'll need to be familiar with when talking to people in the industry you've targeted. I wouldn't count on it for a job, though. I've worked with a lot of clients after they gave up waiting to be discovered.

LinkedIn is relevant in two ways. First, you must have a LinkedIn page, because every headhunter and every corporate recruiter in America goes to LinkedIn to find people and/or to check them out. Your LinkedIn page is strictly business. If you aren't proficient in this area, find someone who is, because this is basically your online presence. This is defense—a base you must have covered.

Personally, I think LinkedIn's best use is as a research tool. This is offense. Use it to find people to talk to. You have a list of target companies; use LinkedIn to find people in those companies, and a way to get to them.

A word of warning. At the beginning of my public speaking career, people would contact me on LinkedIn following a talk I had given, and ask to link to me. Did I know these people? No. Did I want to give offense by refusing, or ignoring them? No. As a result, if you look at my LinkedIn page, you will find that I have over 1100 connections. Do I know all these people? No way! And I don't believe my situation is all that uncommon. You can't trust just because your friend is linked to someone you want to talk with, that they really do know each other. Do the homework! Contact your friend, ask the nature of the relationship, and if warranted, ask for the referral.

Facebook is also a database to mine for referrals and targets.

---

*NOTE:* You must also remember that asking LinkedIn or Facebook contacts for referrals is dangerous. If the relationship isn't there, or if they get the idea that you are asking them to go out of their way, take a risk, or make a commitment to do something—specifically, sponsor you for a job—all is lost, including your friendship!

---

So now you are into the search. This chapter is primarily about planning and starting the search with people you know, and extending to those you don't. For continuation of the search, read the next chapter, "Networking Without Losing Your Friends." You will note that, of necessity, there is some overlap.

Remember this: you must be certain to promise your friends, and the people they refer you to, that you are not coming to them to ask them for a job, or to sponsor you for a job. This is the major difference between networking as you may have known it, and the referral process.

Be careful also not to lie. Goober would say, "I'm not looking for a job, I just want some information . . .." *Liar!! Of* course he's looking for a job! Why else would he be doing this? Learn from Goober. You're just not going to *ask* them for a job. We'll dig into this more deeply in the next chapter.

A final point. One of the things you will learn quickly is that no one returns your phone calls. Don't take this personally. This is largely caused by today's scammers and robocallers. The people you are calling don't mean it personally. It's just that they're busy, and they assume that, if they don't know you, you want something from them, and that's scary. So be certain to prominently mention the name of the person who referred you. It's the referral that will get you a returned call.

I had a client who had had a very successful search, and, during our debriefing meeting, mentioned in passing that everyone he had called and left a message for had called him back. I couldn't believe it. "What was the message," I asked.

He said, "My name is so-and-so, I was referred to you by so-and-so. He said you have valuable information for me. I can be reached on Thursday afternoon, the 19th, between 3 and 5 p.m."

Well. I went to some people who are paid to understand things like this, and asked, "Where is the hook in this phone message?" And, as I expected, the answer was, to the person for whom the message was left, "What valuable information do I have?"

I have to tell you, that isn't a hook that will work on me!

I think there are three hooks. The first is the name of the person doing the referring. It *must* be someone well known to the person the message is for. Second is "what information?" Third, and, to me, most important, is "I can be reached on Thursday afternoon, the 19th, between 3 and 5 p.m."

If you leave me a message with just a name and phone number, I can return your call any time. Any time automatically goes to the bottom of the To Do list. Any time equals never.

But if I know that I can only reach you at a certain time, I'll be sure to call you at that time—even if I'm afraid you might try to sell me a timeshare. It's just human nature!

This is how I would try to approach people:

*1st call: if voicemail, hang up.*

*2nd call: if voicemail, hang up.*

*3rd call: if voicemail, leave a message like the one above.*

Be sure you have access to your phone at the day and time you left in the message.

The client I'm talking about was one from several years ago, and no one since has said that everyone returned their calls. Also, I'm not so sure I would have the courage to use the phrase, ". . . you have valuable information for me." Seems just a bit bold. But I could say ". . . you could be very helpful to me." But I do believe that this is a far more effective way to leave a message for someone than just leaving a name and number.

For the moment, you're just about ready to get started. Read the next chapter, and then get out there and be on your mission.

*Bon chance!* Good hunting!

# CHAPTER 6

# Networking Without
# Losing Your Friends

> *Call it a clan, call it a network, call it a tribe,*
> *call it a family. Whatever you call it, whoever you are,*
> *you need one.*
>
> **— JANE HOWARD, "FAMILIES"**

I have already talked about how more than half of all those looking for a job succeed using informal means, and that many of them create the jobs they take. Now let's get deeply into the process you will use to become one of them.

Although the term most often used for this is networking, I don't like it because it is quickly becoming the credibility equivalent to information interview, that is, there is none. I use networking often in this book because people are familiar with it. I'll use the term referral process here, because that's what it is.

Let's take a look at how our ne'er-do-well friend, Goober goes about getting a job.

Believing that networking is the answer, he enters the search with a club in his hand, and tries to bludgeon people into either hiring him, or sponsoring him for a job. When this fails, he backs up and does it again, harder. When he finally realizes this isn't working, he forswears networking and returns to spending 6 hours a day searching online because, he says, "Networking doesn't work. At least there are jobs online."

Now, you know that trying to get someone else to do your job search for you doesn't work. Let's talk about what does, and the results you might expect—results first.

Earlier I told you that one of my own job searches had taken 10 days, another three days. The record for the shortest job search among the clients I have worked with is also three days. It beat the preceding record of four days. I say this to let you know that this process doesn't have to take a long time.

By now you have selected a target job, company, industry, and geographic location, unless you are using the search to determine the type of job. These will make it possible to conduct a referral search in a short time. And the more tightly focused you are, the shorter the search will be. If you are currently missing one or more of these four, it's likely the search will take longer, but it's the search itself that will give you the answers.

Remember, odd as it sounds, the goal isn't to get a job, it's to get in lots of future hire files—the files that hiring managers keep for the resumés of future hires in their desk drawers, or in their heads, or on their computers.

This is how you get into the files. I'm going to script the referral process here. In doing so, I recognize that I'm setting up an artificial construct, and that it's not likely any referral meeting will follow it exactly, or sometimes even closely. Consider this as a template. Don't even think about memorizing it. In scripting a conversation I'm trying to demonstrate a concept.

So, you have been referred to me by my friend Bob. Here is what I'm thinking:

I don't know who you are;

I don't know what you're doing here;

I'm not sure you won't ask me for a job, even though you said you wouldn't;

I don't know what my role is in this meeting.

In short, I'm uncomfortable. What is it you want from this meeting?" You want four things:

You want to qualify me as a target;

You want information;

You want to get your profile into my future hire file;

You want referrals.

To qualify as a target, I must have at least one problem you can solve. If I have no problems, I am not a target today, but I could easily be a target tomorrow—problems have a way of cropping up without notice. That's why you want to get your profile into my future hire file.

Information means information on the industry—trends, issues, opportunities, challenges, where you fit, how much you can make, and so on. If you make a favorable impression upon me and if I determine that you may be the solution to a present or future problem, be assured your profile will go into my hire file.

Referrals are other people to talk with. I view a referral meeting as successful if you find a problem you can solve, get referred to two or more people, or both.

But before we get into the meeting, let's talk about how you got here.

Bob might have said, "Write Bud a letter and follow up with a phone call to schedule a meeting."

If so, you wrote me a letter saying you were referred to me by Bob, that he thought I might be of considerable help to you as you are in transition and are in the research phase of a job search. Bob thought I could give you valuable information on this industry, and where someone with your skills and abilities might fit in it. You are coming to get information, not to ask me for a job. You'll call me on Tuesday, the 22nd of September, to see when we might get together.

On Tuesday, you called me. You reminded me who you are, you reminded me that you were referred by Bob, that you're coming to get information, not to ask me for a job, and we scheduled a meeting. Then you told me you'd send me a copy of a profile you've put together, so I'd have a better understanding of who you are.

Note that in this process you will use the profile you prepared—not the resumé.

Never send the profile with the letter. If you do, I won't read the letter. I'll see the profile and either send the whole package to human resources, where it will die a protracted and lonely death, or I'll throw it away.

By the way, don't ask if you can send me a copy of your profile. Tell me. You're doing me a favor.

Bob might have told you to send me an email. If so, the letter becomes the script for the email.

He might have said, "Just call him up." If so, the letter becomes the script for the phone call. You must have a script and you must stick to it. In my last job search I found out the hard way what happens when you don't, as you will see a bit farther ahead.

So now, here you are. The meeting will have three phases:

There is an introduction, an information-gathering phase, and a close.

## The Introduction

The introduction is to deal with my issues. Let's start the meeting there. Here are my issues:

I don't know who you are;

I don't know what you're doing here;

I don't necessarily believe you won't ask me for a job;

I don't know what my role is that's going on in my office, and from which there seems to be no escape.

Just about every meeting you attend will start out with my (I'm the person you were referred to) asking, *"So, what can I do for you?"* Everyone will ask that question, because they're not comfortable with the meeting yet, and they want to know what to expect. You will say, "First, let me say thank you for seeing me today. Bob said you might be of considerable help to me, and I just want you to know I appreciate your willingness to take time out of what I'm sure is a busy day. Let me just explain again why I'm here.

"I have this background, blah, blah, blah, I've done these kinds of things, and now I'm in transition, and while I'm looking forward to getting started, the fact is that I'm largely unaware of where my skills and abilities would fit best. You can help me today by answering a bunch of questions about this industry, the business community, maybe give me an evaluation of my skills and some insight into where they'd fit. Let me just say again, I'm not here to ask you for a job. I am here to get the kind of information that will help me put together an effective job search. Is that okay?"

*"Well, I guess so."*

Now, you've told me who you are, you've told me what you're doing here, you've told me again that you're not going to ask me for a job, and you've told me what my role is—I'm the answer guy. You've dealt with my issues. You've given me the agenda.

Time out. I have taught clients these words for years, and most clients like them. If you can use my words and be yourself that's fine. If you can't, be yourself, with a couple of exceptions. There are two places in the above introduction where you need to use my words.

The first is, "Let me just explain again why I'm here."

This tells the listener that the agenda is forthcoming. The majority of people entering a meeting want to know the agenda, especially if they believe they are at risk.

The other words you need to use are at the end. "Is that okay?" You need verbal buy-in from the person you're meeting with in order to move ahead. The only way to get that is to ask for it.

Goober's approach to this is, "I'll wing it." As a result, suddenly confronted with someone whose enthusiasm about this meeting is decidedly less than his, he forgets to say thank you, he sums up his career in about 10 seconds, he says he's not looking for a job ("So why are you here? Is this a hobby?") and finishes in about 20 seconds.

I haven't researched this, but I believe time is as important as covering the bases here. As the person you're meeting, I'm processing a lot of information on the fly as you speak, trying to understand and get comfortable simultaneously. You need to give me time to get used to the idea of this meeting. But if I start looking at my watch, it's probably a sign that you can move on.

At any rate, we have now dealt with the issues.

I would anticipate that the introduction will take somewhere between two and 10 minutes, depending on the level of response by the person you're talking with.

## Information Gathering

There is a very specific order to this phase. First, we will talk about my industry, then my company, then your profile, and last, a job or jobs.

We go in this order to give me time to get used to this conversation, and to build my comfort level in talking with you. If you go directly to the job now, I'm going to get nervous.

Which brings us to an interesting point.

There are two ways to handle just about anything that comes up in one of these meetings. One is to ignore it—it isn't important; it will go away. The other is to maximize it.

Any time I look uncomfortable, that is a maximizing situation. If you ignore my discomfort, it will only grow in the dark under the desk and kill you before you leave. If you say or ask anything that causes me to flinch—if I show any sign of discomfort—everything stops.

"Let me back up for a moment. A little while ago I said I was not here to ask you for a job. I meant that. If I'm going to put together a successful job search, there's an awful lot of information I need to get. The only way I know to get it is to ask questions. Please bear with me—when I leave here today, I will not have asked you for a job. Is that okay?"

Once again, you must ask, "Is that okay?" If you don't, it won't be!

Now, when you drag that fear out from under the desk and start waving it around at me like a dead flounder, it goes away. You've gotten it out into the open and dealt with it. But if I look uncomfortable again five minutes from now, you'd better start waving that flounder around again—any time I look uncomfortable, deal with it. If you don't, the meeting will get ugly.

All that said, now you can ask any question you want about the industry I'm in. Anything is valid. Is it growing? Is it shrinking? Is it consolidating, the way banking and healthcare have done? What effect does winter have on it? China? Anything.

Included in these questions, though, will be probes. Remember, you're here to find a problem. If I don't have a problem, I'm not a target.

Do you think I'm going to volunteer problems? One of two things is the case at this point. Either I've decided you are who you say you are, and you're not going to ask me for a job, in which case I'm on cruise control—I'm not even thinking about problems; or I'm still waiting for the other shoe to drop—I'm not volunteering anything.

Either way, if you want problems, you're going to have to dig for them.

At first hearing, this thought tends to make people uncomfortable, so let's take time out to address this.

Some people misunderstand, and hear that I am teaching extreme militance, carrying on an interrogation that leaves the person they're meeting with bruised, beaten and vowing revenge. Nothing could be further from the truth. That would be *exactly* the wrong approach. If you do what I'm telling you, and exercising common sense, you will come across as a self-confident seeker of wisdom and truth, someone the listener can respect and enjoy talking with. You are appealing to their knowledge and expertise, and to their willingness to help others without going out of their way. And you may well make lasting friendships.

Let's take my client Bill's experience, for example. One thing you'll notice is that he was much more direct than what I have been advocating.

Bill was a client who had a dramatically successful search, creating an excellent job for himself at a substantial raise. He left that company in mid-December 2008. You may remember what was happening then. The economy had just plunged off a cliff. Layoffs abounded.

By the end of January 2009—six weeks later—he was pending employment in six companies, and went to work for one of them. This was his search.

He would be referred to a decision-maker and would meet with that person and say, "Let me explain why I'm here. I'm looking for someone with a problem." Showing his profile to that person, he would continue, "Here are the kinds of problems I like to solve, and, as you can see, I'm pretty good at solving them. I *love* these kinds of problems! Who would you know who would have these kinds of problems?"

That was the whole meeting! And it netted him six companies in six weeks. How? Because it was obvious to those with whom he spoke that he was going to be successful in the search, so they needed to take a very good look at him. He was unstoppable. We'll come back to this point.

Okay, back to the referral process. When we left the meeting, you were going to look for problems.

So how do you probe? You might try questions like these:

"Tell me, what do you see going on in the hot dip galvanizing industry right now that will have a positive effect on a company like this? Is that something you're experiencing now? What kinds of challenges does that create for you? Is that a problem? How big a problem is that?"

"What else is going on that's positive? Is that something you're experiencing? What kinds of challenges does that produce? Is that a problem? How big a problem is that?"

"What is going on in the industry that's a threat? Is that something you're dealing with now? How big a problem is that?"

"Where do you see hot dip galvanizing in five years? Is that where you want this company to be? What could keep that from happening? Is that something you're experiencing now? How big a problem is that?"

Note that, while discussing the industry, we are also talking about the company, unannounced.

Let's move on.

"I appreciate your comments about the industry. What I'd like to do now is use this company as a model of the industry—is that a reasonable thing to do?"

*"Yup, I guess it is."*

"Great!"

Or, *"Nope. I don't think we're typical!"*

"Well that's interesting! Why not?"

Now, whatever my response is to "why not," it is useful information. Write it down.

Regardless of why not, you will say, "I can certainly understand that. What I'd like to do for this conversation is—ignore that." Now I'm a model anyway.

As was the case with asking about the industry, any question is valid. "Is the company growing? Shrinking? Why? What opportunities do you see coming up? What challenges do you face?" And so forth. (Remember, if a question you ask causes me to look or act uncomfortable, start swinging that flounder around—fast!)

At this point we have discussed both my industry and my company. Now it is time to deal with your profile.

Where is it?

If it was sitting on my desk or my computer screen when you walked in, fine. If not, I've lost it. You can depend on one out of every three people you meet with to misplace your profile by the time you get to them. If it isn't available, now you'll have to deal with that.

"I had some questions I wanted to ask you about the profile I sent you, but it appears that you haven't gotten it. I have an extra copy with me. Would you like it?"

Ninety-nine out of 100 people will say they'd like a copy, if for no other reason than to be polite.

Number 100 will say, *"Oh, I don't think that will be necessary."* And your meeting is just about over. But you knew that, because this guy hasn't been cooperating from the beginning. You're probably only about 10 minutes into the meeting, and it won't last 10 more minutes. But that's OK. If he doesn't want you there, you don't want to be there.

If I'm among the other 99, watch what happens when you hand me the profile.

I'll do one of two things with it. I'll either glance at it and lay it aside with some innocuous comment or I'll start reading it.

This moment is useful in determining your progress in the meeting. If I start reading, you have probably made an impression upon me. I'm more interested in seeing who you are than when we started.

If I lay it aside unread, the end of the meeting is in sight. I'm perfectly comfortable in my ignorance of what the profile says. I'm not playing the game. I'm wondering when and how this will end.

If I start reading, that's your cue to become a statue. Otherwise you're a distraction. When I'm finished, I might ask a question, I might make a comment, or simply lay it aside.

If I have just read it, you say, "I have a few questions about my profile. Could we go back to that for a minute?"

*"Sure,"* I'll say, and I'll pick it back up.

If it was sitting on my desk when you walked in, assume I've read it. If it is apparent that I didn't read it we have to deal with that.

"I'd really appreciate your taking a few minutes to read that, because I have some serious questions about it."

Now I'm stuck. I have to read it. There's a test coming—*serious* questions. So, I'll read it. I may not want to, but I'll do it.

At this point, one way or another—either voluntarily or under duress, I've read the profile.

You must understand that there is more art to this process than science. As you are probably aware, any time people get involved things can get messy. At the same time, human nature, in general, is predictable. What we hope to do is capitalize on the general rules of human nature. Now it's time to ask some questions about the profile. "In reading the profile, is there anything that stands out? Is there anything that causes you to think, 'Here's someone I wouldn't mind having a conversation with?"

"Well, yes. The fact that you reduced rework by more than 30 percent."

"Why does that get your attention?"

"Rework is a major expense for us."

"I see. At this point I'd have to say that hot dip galvanizing is where I want to be. It seems maybe reducing rework is something I should emphasize. Would you agree?"

"You bet—that's a big deal."

"What else stands out?"

"You seem to have been quite successful overall."

"Thank you. Tell me, is there anything missing? Anything that you don't see, so you throw it away?"

"Yes. You don't have an MBA."

"So, are you telling me that without an MBA I'll never work in hot dip galvanizing?"

"Yes."

"Why is that so important? How can I overcome that"?

If I say, "You can't overcome that," we've just hit a dead end.

Any time you hit a dead end, your answer is the same.

"I appreciate your honesty in saying that. How would you use this background, these skills in this industry? In the business community?"

Now let's talk about what you don't ask.

"How do you like the profile? How would you change it?"

If you ask, you've asked. Now you'll have to sit there politely while they rewrite the entire thing!

In discussing profiles, I said that the format confuses people. It makes them uncomfortable. They do not see it as a profile.

They see it as a resumé, and they don't like it. And now you have just given them the opportunity to fix it.

And what will you do when they finally hand it back to you and say, *"When you get it fixed, why don't you send me a copy?"*

You're not fixing it. It did what it was supposed to do.

Don't go there. The only questions you ask are what stands out and what's missing, with follow-up questions to gain clarity.

If they do get carried away with the profile, just tell them that you didn't mean for it to be a resumé. You just wanted to demonstrate your successes using skills you believe are transferable, so you can find your place in corporate America.

At this point we've been through the profile, and I've probably learned a few more things about you.

"Let me ask you," you will say, "based on what you know about me at this point—what you've seen in the profile, what I've told you about myself—where would someone with this sort of background, these kinds of skills, fit best in a company similar to this one?"

Now, what you have just asked me is, "Where would I fit in your company?" But you can't ask it that way. If you do, I know what the next question is. "When do I start?"

You're making the question as theoretical as you possibly can. "Where would *someone*, with this *sort* of background, these *kinds* of skills . . . ." Keep in mind, however, that some serious flounder-swinging may be necessary at this point.

"So, where would someone with these kinds of skills fit in an organization like this?"

*"Well, I don't think you would."*

Dead end.

"I appreciate your honesty. Why do you say that? How would you use these skills and abilities in this industry? In the business community?"

Remember, any time you hit a dead end, that's your response.

*"Well, in this company I think you'd be the operations manager."*

"That's fascinating. Why do you say that? What skills specifically would I use in that job? What kinds of problems would I solve? Do you have someone in that job now?"

*"Yep, we sure do."*

"Terrific! Profile that person for me. What makes him good? Is it skill? Is it work ethic? What is it?"

"If he were to walk in here tomorrow morning and resign, do you think I'd be qualified to do his job?"

Now, that question makes clients a bit nervous. It seems that you're walking right up to the line you swore you wouldn't cross, and you're about to *jump over* it!

Not so. I just put you in that job. You asked where someone like you would fit, I said operations manager, and now you're asking if you would be qualified. That isn't likely to upset me. If it does, deal with it.

It is also unlikely that I'll say no. But it's possible.

*"Nope—I don't think you would."*

"I appreciate your honesty. Why do you say that . . .?

I think you get the picture. More likely the response will be:

*"Yeah, I think you could do that job."*

Well, isn't that cool! You have just been qualified for a job in corporate America! From this point on, you can say, "I've been told that I'd be qualified for an operations management position."

But wait—do you think that's the only job you can do in a company? Of course not. So why stop there?

Keep asking. "Where else would you see someone with my skills and abilities fitting in?" Keep going until I run out of jobs. It may not be until we get to the third one that I slap myself on the forehead and say, *"Where have you been? We need you!"*

I worked with a client who had degrees in math and data science, with plans to be a data analyst, and had zero postgrad experience. The first person he was referred to was the senior vice president of a bank. The client's first question following the introduction was, "How do you use data analysis here?" The vice president's answer was, "We don't, but we have a lot of data and I'd like to find a way to use it." From that answer came a meeting scheduled with the vice president and his financial and IT leaders to see how my client could help them.

So, at this point we've been through the introduction, we covered the industry, my company, you've asked about the profile, and you've been qualified for at least one job

Remember, you're still looking for a problem.

The search that took me ten days brought me to Richmond, Virginia. Some things happened in that search that I believe can be helpful to you, so here's the story.

In May of 1991, I was trying to make a go of career consulting on my own, and it wasn't working. I was good at providing the service, but I wasn't good at marketing. I woke up one morning, and my first conscious thought of the day was, "I've got to find someone who will pay me to do this."

I called a friend who owned a small corporate outplacement firm, and said to him, "Paul, I know you can't afford to hire me, and I'm not complaining, but I need to find someone who can! But I don't know who's out there. I don't even know if I fit!

I've got to get out there and talk to some people, and you have to help me!"

He replied, *"You're absolutely right. That's how I got into this business. Call these four people and tell them I told you to call."*

So, my search started with a phone call, and I got four names. That's not bad.

It took me a few years before I realized that, if I'd had the good sense to go sit down with Paul, I'd have gotten *at least* those four names—they came right off the top of his head—and I probably would have gotten a whole lot of information that I didn't even think to ask for on the phone. How dumb is that?

I've mentioned this before. It is of critical importance to meet with people. If you don't—if you try to do this by phone—all you will get is what's on the top of their heads. I have a very low opinion of phone meetings, especially with people you don't know. I've had a couple of those, and they were a total waste of time. This is a relationship game. You do not build relationships on the phone.

Still, four names aren't bad.

I called the first name on the list. He was the managing director of the Washington, DC, office of America's largest outplacement company. His first words were, "Paul who?" He wouldn't see me. Like an idiot, I tried to explain who Paul was. Much better to have just said, "I'm sorry. I have the wrong number." If you have to explain who the referring person is, it's not a referral.

I called the second name on the list. She worked for a regional outplacement firm. Her name was Judy. We scheduled an appointment.

I called the third name. I went to see him, and it was a total waste of time. He was an idiot. It didn't occur to me for about a year that he was Goober. I could have replaced him! I missed what might have been a great opportunity because it hadn't occurred to me to look for a Goober to replace.

I called the fourth name. She refused to see me, told me I was wasting her time, and asked that I never call back again. Sometimes you'll get those.

So, I had gone from four names to one in short order.

I went to see my new friend Judy.

We had scheduled a 45-minute meeting. We talked for an hour and a half. At the end of an hour and a half, she said, *"Your next step is to meet with our Director of Professional Staff, and I'll set that up for you."*

Sound good? It was unbelievably good, given the idiot I had made of myself on the phone when I called her.

I called her immediately after the first guy refused to see me, because I knew that if I didn't do it then, I never would. I said to Judy word for word what I had said to the first guy, because it was a script. She agreed immediately to see me.

I was so surprised that I forgot what I was doing.

Now, I'm the guy who teaches this stuff. The truth is that I didn't believe it would work for me. When it did, I was so shocked that I forgot about the script and just started babbling. She listened to me for about 20 seconds and concluded that I was hoping she would hire me while I was sitting in her office (she was right!). When she figured that out, everything changed.

Judy said, *"Wait a minute! If you're looking for a job, don't waste my time. If you want information, come see me and I'll do what I can. But if it's a job you're after, forget it! We are not going to hire you. We don't need you. We have no interest in you."* Fortunately for me, she finished off with, *"So what will it be?"* (That's all a quote, by the way!)

I said in about as trembling a voice as I've ever heard, "Information?"

She said, *"Okay, come see me."*

Now, let's look at this for a moment. What was my purpose in calling Judy? To schedule an appointment. Did we do that? Yes. What happened then? I kept talking. And then? I almost lost the appointment.

Your goal in contacting people is to schedule an appointment. Once you have done that, there is nothing you can say further that will help you. There is *plenty* you can say that will hurt you! Once you have achieved the goal, hang up. Do it politely but get the heck off the phone!

When I stepped into her office, we had established well beyond doubt that there was no job there for Bud.

An hour and a half later, *"Your next step is to meet with our Director of Professional Staff. And I'll set that up for you."*

Not bad.

Two things happened in my meeting with Judy that I believe contributed to that result. First was chemistry. Within 15 minutes we were pals, having a great time. The second was an event that occurred, and I can no longer remember when it occurred or what we were talking about.

I found myself leaning across her desk, pointing at her, and saying, *"This* is what I am going to do. I hope I can find somebody who will pay me to do it! But if nobody will pay me, I'll do it in churches on Sunday afternoons. I'll do it in my basement. This isn't a job for me—it's a *calling!"*

Well, that was definitely a defining moment for me. I didn't realize the truth of those words until I had about half of them out. I got goose bumps. I still do when I say them.

The impact on Judy was a whole lot bigger. I never asked, but I haven't the slightest doubt that at that moment I stopped being *"Bud Whitehouse, friend of Paul's, maybe I can help him, and maybe not, and who really cares,"* and instantly became Bud Whitehouse, *". . . player. I think we'd better see who he's going to play for!"*

I became unstoppable.

Here we come to the most important rule of all:

---

*You must be unstoppable!*

---

Remember Bill? He was also unstoppable. The bad news is that if you are stoppable, people will stop you. It's human nature. But if you're unstoppable, they'll either get the heck out of your way, or they'll join you to be on the winning team!

Judy chose the winning team.

Think of it this way—*if I conclude that you are either going to be my greatest asset as my employee, or my worst nightmare as my competitor's employee I need to stop and take a serious look at you.*

"I'm going to help somebody make a lot of money. Or maybe save a lot, or maybe both, and I'm going to have a lot of fun doing it. I don't know who that person is yet, but when I find him, I'll know!"

Now that is somebody you had better take a serious look at. He's either going to make you a fortune or put you out of business.

For some reason, this is the one concept in the job hunt that everyone misses.

When I was in high school, my sophomore English teacher was also the wrestling coach. For a whole school year, every Friday he told me, "Whitehouse, next year you're going out for wrestling." So, I did. But I wasn't a wrestler. I *hated* it. I wrestled to not lose. You can't do that. When you are only trying not to lose, you get killed by the other guy, because he's out to *win*.

Neither can you look for a job in such a way as not to lose.

You must be unstoppable. If you take nothing else away from this, this alone will make you successful.

After telling me about the director, Judy said, *"You go home and call him, but I'll have already talked to him and given him your* resumé.*"*

I went home and called him. We scheduled a 45-minute meeting.

His name was Rick. I went to see Rick, and we talked for two hours. At the end of two hours, he said, *"I'd hire you in a heartbeat if I had the need or the budget. I don't have either one right now. Would you like to be a stringer?"*

Now a stringer is not an employee. He is not on the payroll. He is like a temp. He is usually doing something else for a living, and when the company needs more people for a project, they call him up. I was already a stringer for my friend Paul.

In that business, you can't string for two companies, so I had a decision to make.

On the one hand was Rick—Ph.D. in Operations Research and Senior Vice President for this regional outplacement firm whose reputation for quality of service made them exalted in the industry; not the largest, but—most people in the business seemed to think—the best. Rick oversaw all the services the firm provided in the Washington, D.C. metropolitan area. I had just hit the big time!

On the other hand, there was Paul, who worked out of his house.

I said, "Thanks a lot for the offer; I really appreciate it, but no. If there's a way to do this full time, I'm going to find it. I just don't know what it is yet."

He said, *"Well, I have a friend. A couple of months ago he had a problem. I don't know if he still does, but if he does, I think you're the solution. Call Walt Limbach and tell him I told you to call."*

Now, a couple of things happened in my meeting with Rick. First was the event in which I pointed across the desk and said, "This is what I am going to do." When I saw the effect it had on Judy, I memorized it on the spot. When I said it, word for word, to Rick, it had the same effect. When I said it again, word for word, to Walt, it had the same effect. The point is, when you find something that works, keep doing it.

The second thing was the end of our meeting. Rick said, *"If I could hire you, I would. I can't. Would you like to be a stringer?"*

I said, "No."

He said, *"I have a friend."*

What do you think would have happened if I'd said, "Yes"? I'd have been a stringer. Strung out by now.

Rick was looking out for Rick. What a surprise! Only after he found he had nothing to gain did he think of Walt, who I later found out was his best friend.

Do you think Rick is unusual? Not at all.

What this means is that, when you set foot into Rick's office you had better have already given serious thought as to what you are willing to do, and what you are not willing to do; because Rick will be offering more than what you have, but less than what you want. And I'm not saying your answer should be "no." You just need to have already thought about it because it will be difficult to do that objectively while sitting in Rick's office.

So, I called Walt.

He came on the phone, and I said, "My name is Bud Whitehouse. I was referred to you by Rick. He said he didn't know if you still have a problem, but that if you do, I'm probably the solution."

Now that still seems bold to me. And the truth is that, as I was saying those words, I was trembling! But I also knew exactly what I was doing. I was quoting Rick. If Walt had gotten upset, I'd have laid those words at Rick's feet so fast it would have made him dizzy.

Walt didn't get upset. He just said, *"Well, I think you should come talk to me."* We scheduled a 45-minute meeting.

And then what do you think I did?

I hung up! I'm learning!

I went to see Walt at ten o'clock on a Friday morning.

For the first two hours, we talked about the Marine Corps. Walt is a retired Lieutenant Colonel and jet pilot.

He's insane.

I spent a year attached to the Marines, so, *"Semper Fi."*

We talked about Vietnam. He flew over it, I walked across it. We talked about outplacement, about the giants of outplacement and what they had done for it.

We finally got to his situation. It turned out that he had an office in Richmond, Virginia, that was growing slowly and painfully. He had a guy who did what I do commuting the 90 miles each way between Northern Virginia, where we were, and Richmond, working his way into full time in Richmond as the office grew.

Two months prior to my meeting with Walt, that guy dropped dead of a heart attack. Now *there's* a problem. It was a *big* problem. He had a bunch of clients in Richmond, no one really taking care of them, and a couple of them were talking about suing him.

Walt tells people that at this point I turned to him and asked, "Walt, how long until *you* have a heart attack?" He says his next thought was, *"I wonder if this guy can start on Monday?"* And I had a job.

The fact is, I don't remember being quite that blunt, but he says that's what happened. I don't necessarily recommend asking when the other person might have a heart attack, but it certainly worked on Walt!

Part of the time I was in Vietnam, I worked for a doctor that the Marines all called "Dr. Squeeze" behind his back, because, they said, no matter what was wrong with you, he would squeeze it and ask, "Does that hurt?"

That's what you're doing here. You are out to find a problem, and when you do, squeeze! "How long can this go on before you're losing real money?" I think "how long until you have a heart attack" qualifies as a squeeze.

I believe that I was nearly hired by the time I walked into Walt's office. I never asked him, but I suspect that within 30 seconds of our telephone conversation, he was on the phone to Rick, saying, "Who is this Whitehouse guy, and why have you inflicted him upon me?" And Rick probably told him just who that Whitehouse guy was. The only thing Walt needed to know by the time we met was whether he would like me and trust me working in an office 90 miles away. So, we talked about the Marines. We bonded.

That is finding the problem. Now let's get back to the referral process itself.

Another question you'll ask as part of information gathering is this one:

"How much money do you think I can make doing this?"

In the employment interview, you never talk about money. In the referral meeting you always ask about money—it's part of the research you're doing.

I worked once with a young man who was entering corporate America for the first time. When he came to me, he thought he could make a salary in the lower thirties. By asking the question he found he could make over $60,000. If he hadn't asked, he would have gone with the first person who would offer what he expected.

"How much can I make doing this? What about in a larger company? What about in a smaller company? What about in a different aspect of the industry? What about in a different industry? What about twenty miles up the road?"

That is how you establish your market value. And it is much more accurate than looking up tables on the internet.

So that is information gathering. Properly done, it should take an absolute minimum of twenty minutes, but it could take hours. My meeting with Walt, scheduled for 45 minutes, began at 10 am. I left at 6 pm.

Let's go on to phase three, the close.

## The Close

The close has three questions.

The first question is, "If you were me, how would you proceed in a search like this one?"

**Important note:** In asking this question, you are also saying that you're looking for a job. In the introduction to our meeting, Goober said, "I'm just looking for information, I'm not looking for a job," and now he has just walked all over his tongue, hasn't he! And he has lost all hope of credibility. Never say you aren't looking for a job. There is a world of difference between, "I'm not here to ask you for a job," and, "I'm not looking for a job!"

Back to our story.

Everyone will give you the same answer, *"Oh, I'd do just what you're doing. You have to get out there and talk to people!"*

That isn't why you asked the question.

What's going on in my head when I give you that answer is, *"Gee, if I had to get a job, what would I do? Who would I talk to?"*

*That* is why you asked the question. Question one is there to cause the answer to question two to surface at about the time you ask it. Question number two is, "Who do you know who I could talk to further about this?"

The only problem here is that, asked this way, the question is fatal.

Goober asked, "Who do you know," and was rewarded with this response: *"Gee, uh, let me think about that, and I'll get back to you."*

Now Goober's meeting is over, and he goes his way.

Days pass. No phone call. Finally, he calls me and the receptionist tells me he's on the phone.

"Take a message," I say.

What is going through my head right now is guilt. "I didn't do what I said I would do. But there's still time. If I can just come up with a couple of people, I'll call him back, and he'll never know I didn't do what I said I'd do. 'Take a message.'"

So now do I think about who Goober should call? No. I've bought time. I go back to doing what I was doing.

Days pass, and he calls me again. I immediately tell the receptionist to take a message, and from that moment until one of us dies or leaves town, I will avoid Goober like the plague.

I can't speak with him without being embarrassed. He knows I didn't do what I said I'd do. Well, there is a simple solution to that little problem. I won't speak with Goober at all. If I see him in a store, I'll *run* the other way.

Goober has just burned a contact, and it's his own fault. He asked me a question I couldn't answer easily and made me lie.

The question was too big. The question can't be one global, "who do you know?" It must be a lot of little, "who do you knows."

"Earlier you said I'd be qualified to be operations manager. Are you responsible for that part of the company?"

*"Nope. Charlie is."*

"Oh, Charlie! I'll bet Charlie could be helpful to me. How can we arrange for me to meet with Charlie?"

Or, *"Yes, I'm responsible for that crew."*

"Fantastic! I'll bet there are a few people in that group who could be helpful to me. Who do you think we should start with? What about other people on the management team? Who do you think I could speak with there? What about your vendors? What about your clients? What about your CPA firm? Do they specialize in this industry? Who could I speak with there? What about your attorney? What about your competition?"

It is easy for me to identify whom you should speak with if you help me by breaking the question into little pieces. Otherwise you can watch my brain freeze and my eyes glaze over.

The second question is actually questions number two.

In material I had to work with when I worked for someone else, the last question in the meeting was, "Would you mind if I were to keep you apprised of my progress in the search?"

Have you ever seen *Gone with the Wind*? Perhaps you'll remember a famous line from that movie.

"Frankly, Scarlett, I don't give a damn!"

That's what pops into my head every time I hear that stupid question. Oddly, I don't think the person you're talking with will get it. He'll say, *"Oh, no problem."* And you won't have a problem.

Not until you call him. I will guarantee you that whatever he happens to be doing at the time of your call, including playing solitaire on his computer, will be of greater importance to him than being kept apprised of your progress.

I would ask instead, and did in the search that brought me to Richmond, "You know, as I talk with more people, as I get more information, I expect that I'll have a couple of questions that I'll wish I had thought to ask you today. If I do have more questions, and, again, I promise not to abuse the privilege, may I give you a call?"

When you say, "Again, I promise not to abuse the privilege," you remind me that, although you've been sitting here for the better part of an hour, and you've had a golden opportunity to hound me for a job, you told me you wouldn't, and you've honored your commitment. The trust you're asking for now is a whole lot less than the trust you've already honored. *"Call me any time."*

With my agreement for you to call, the meeting is over.

And that is the referral meeting. The way it's presented here, it may seem like you're using a machine gun on the other person, but in real life it becomes a conversation, because a question generates an answer, which generates another question, *et cetera.* But it does resemble a military exercise. You know what you want to get, you go get it, you establish a *relationship* along the way, and you get out. Properly done it should take at least 45 minutes.

Now let's discuss referral hierarchy.

There are only three ways you can be referred—up, across, and down. We'll begin with "up."

I, Bud, cost accountant, come to you, Ms. Big, Vice President of Finance, and say, "Ma'am, I met a young accountant the other day who might be the solution to the problem you were talking about in the staff meeting."

Now, your first thought as Ms. Big, VP of Finance, is, "Whitehouse, you're darn near 60 years old and you're still a cost accountant! What could possibly make you think I'd have any interest in anyone you would have in mind?"

This is called a suggestion. Suggestions rarely work. About the only time you can depend on a suggestion is when there is also a relationship involved that minimizes the difference in social standing between the parties.

Now let's consider "across."

I, Bud, Vice President of Marketing, come to you, Susan, Vice President of Finance, and say, "You know, Susan, I met a young accountant the other day who might be the solution to the problem you were talking about in the Executive Committee meeting."

This is called a peer referral. It works every time.

Now let's look at "down."

I, Mr. Whitehouse, Chairman and CEO, come to you, Susan, Vice President of Finance, and say, "You know, you might want to have a chat with my son-in-law."

This is called a command. A command has never failed.

This should tell you the level at which you need to be working—at least one level above what you want, preferably two levels above. It is much easier to be referred down than up.

Now we need to talk about what to do after your meeting with Mr. Big. How are you going to say thank you to this nice person who has helped you?

Sadly, it never occurred to Goober to do this. The meeting's over and he's outta there, probably never to be seen again. Or, if it did occur to him he just dashed off a quick email and moved on.

In doing this, Goober missed out on one of the greatest opportunities ever to cement a relationship—the thank you card.

While you are in Mr. Big's office look for clues, either in the trappings of the office or in what he says, as to what he likes. My office has prints of sailing ships. I love them. So you might ask me, to confirm, "I see the prints. You must be a sailing fan?" If I am, you will know. If not, you will also know. Because I am, we'll assume I answered your question in the affirmative.

Now, after our meeting, you will go to an art or art supply shop, or gallery, a museum, a printer, somewhere you might find a card with a sailing ship on the front. In the card you will thank me for seeing you, refer to any parts of the meeting that really helped you or that you enjoyed, tell me that you have done what I suggested (after you have) and tell me your next steps. All this in handwriting. Mr. Big will be astonished. And happy!

This is a lost art. If you formed any sort of positive relationship, this will cement it. If you didn't, it won't hurt.

Don't send a letter. Never send an email. There is no relationship in either of these. The card is magic.

A final note. In the employment interview you never take notes, because, as the hiring manager, I will assume that what you are writing down are my words *verbatim*, to be used against me in a court of law if I don't hire you. What do you think that will do to the chemistry? But in the referral meeting, you always take notes, for two reasons. First, it is likely that what you are hearing is important and worth writing down to keep. Second, and at least as important, you show respect by taking notes. Presumably, what I'm saying is important, or you wouldn't be coming to sit at my feet and gain the benefit of my wisdom. Always ask permission first, but know that it will very likely be granted.

These are the basics of the referral process. But the bottom line is:

---

Esse Nequit
*(Be Unstoppable!)*

---

## CHAPTER 7

# The Employment Interview: Strategy and Tactics

*"All men can see these tactics whereby I conquer,*
*but what none see is the strategy out of which*
*victory is evolved."*

**– SUN TZU**

Now let's talk about the actual employment interview. No matter where you have lived and worked, you have probably concluded that the employment interview is an adversarial process.

Here's what the hiring manager is thinking about the interview:

1. I have a problem, or I wouldn't be hiring. I don't like problems.

2. I'm uncomfortable with the interview process, because I've had little or no training in how to interview, and it's worked out poorly on occasion in the past.
3. I'm at risk and you could be a mistake. You could be the one who sinks my career.

Years ago I had a client who had been the executive vice president of a Fortune 500 company, who, at this point in our conversation, said, "Absolutely right! I may miss a good one, but I'll *never* hire a bad one!"

Let's look at the logic behind this for a moment. Here are the steps the manager goes through, after the three above:

1. When I'm at risk, I don't play offense, I play defense. I don't think, "I'm going out there and find Superman to do this job," I circle the wagons.
2. How do I play defense in the interview?
3. *Kill 'em all, and let God sort it out. I'll hire the survivor!*

Here's the point: if I'm hiring, I'm trying to find out what's wrong with you, so I don't have to take the risk of hiring you, so I can get on to the next candidate for employment, and not hire him either.

See? There *is* no logic behind this. If I'm hiring, I'm trying to kill you. Terrific. Now let's look at your part in this highly flawed process.

It becomes your job as the candidate for employment to show the good, hide the bad, and get the offer. That's bad enough, but it can easily get worse.

Let's take a look at our friend, Goober, and how he approaches the interview.

When Goober was a child, he obeyed his parents most of the time. Why? Fear. And maybe respect. At an early age, Goober has learned the meaning of the word consequences. When he starts school, Goober learns on day one to obey the teacher. Same reason. After cementing the lesson with a number of teachers, Goober is ready to play his part in corporate America. Having gotten an interview, he approaches the hiring manager's office.

But an odd thing happens when he enters that office. A tiny switch flips in Goober's brain, and he suddenly reverts back to that student-child, thinking, "If I behave myself, and I answer the questions correctly, and I please this person, I may be rewarded with a job! And I need a job. I need this job!" In the hall outside the manager's office, Goober was the candidate. Now he sits down, assuming the electric chair position, and has become the supplicant—the beggar. The hiring manager doesn't hire beggars.

Coming through the door, Goober gave the hiring manager power and authority he didn't have until Goober arrived and gave it to him. And now, in this adversarial process they're about to go through, Goober has to fight against the power he just gave the manager!

This isn't likely to work.

Now let's talk about how you won't be anything like Goober, and you will ace the interview. But first, let's look at another environment for a moment.

You're feeling unwell. Downright sick. So, you go to the doctor's office. Which of you has the problem? You do—you're sick.

Which of you has the potential solution to the problem? The doctor.

Which of you is asking all the questions? The doctor.

Why? So he can figure out what the problem is, and fix it.

And in this question and answer period, who's in charge? The doctor.

Why? Because he's the expert. He's going to solve your problem.

Now let's apply this to the employment interview. There you are in the hiring manager's office.

Which of you has the problem? The hiring manager. Remember, hiring is only done to solve problems. Perhaps you're thinking you have the problem, because you need to find a job. Read on.

Which of you has the potential solution to the problem? You do—the candidate.

So, who's in charge?

You need to be the one in charge. You should be the one asking the questions.

Maybe you've worked with consultants in the past. What is a consultant? Someone who has knowledge and expertise in a particular area of business.

If I'm in business and I have a problem, I call in a consultant.

The consultant does not come in congratulating me for my good sense in calling him and telling me all the wonderful things he's going to do for me. He comes in asking questions. "What are you trying to accomplish? What kinds of problems are you having? How long have you had them? What have you done about them?"

He's asking the same questions the doctor did. And for the same reason—he needs to find out what the problem is before he can fix it.

So, I explain the problem, and he tells me whether or not he can help me, and, if so, how.

Why shouldn't the employment interview be like that?

The bottom line is that, in the employment interview,

---

*You must be the doctor or the consultant.*

---

You're the one asking the questions. You may be the solution to my problem, but you can't be the solution until you know what the problem is. And you certainly won't find out by just answering my questions. Goober goes into the interview blathering about all the wonderful things he's done, hoping some of it will be on target. Not you.

Now, let's look at how the hiring manager approaches the interview.

He's acting on some thoughts or assumptions that he's not even thinking consciously about. One of them is, "This could be win-win. I win, 'cause I'm gonna win—I'm the boss. I win because I hire somebody smart. You win because you're the smart person I hire. Or it could be win-lose. I win. I win because I don't hire a dummy. You lose, because you're a dummy."

It's more likely to be win-lose than it is to be win-win, because he's going to interview several people, but he's only going to hire one. Statistically, the likelihood is that any given interview will be win-lose.

He's not even thinking lose-win or lose-lose. Those aren't options, but they are fears in the back of his head. It is these fears that drive the kill'em all process he uses to interview. The truth is that he's probably not consciously thinking win-win or win-lose either, but he's acting on the thought.

In his ignorance, having had either no training or abysmal training in how to do this, or acting on flawed experience, he thinks he knows what questions to ask that will tell him whether you're going to be any good at this job or not. In short, he's going to play Twenty Questions with you.

Now as the student-child, there is no way Goober will win Twenty Questions. But you will, because, unlike Goober, you will be the consultant or the doctor.

So now we have a situation where the hiring manager's coming into the interview, ready to ask questions. You're coming into the interview as the consultant, ready to ask questions. This could get interesting.

So, you walk through the door into his office, shake hands, and establish that, yes, it is a nice day out, no, not too hot, but no doubt there's still a little hot weather left, and, no, you didn't have any trouble finding a place to park.

This is called setting the candidate at ease. Your interviewer was told by Human Resources that he should do that, so now he's gotten it out of the way, and he can get on with the interview.

What's his first question?

### "Tell Me About Yourself."

This is likely to be the first question in the interview. Two kinds of people ask it—those who know what they're doing, and those who don't. The odds are enormous that your interviewer falls into the category of those who don't know what they're doing.

If he's in that category, "Tell me about yourself" seems to work. It's a social question, fits in with the weather and the parking spaces, then you'll say some stuff, and then he can start asking real questions. Does he know what he wants to hear from you, or what he expects to hear? No—he's just using the question as a vehicle to get from one place to another.

If he knows what he's doing, what he's looking for is a concise summary of who you are relative to your reason for sitting in that chair right now.

Goober will answer "Tell me about yourself" with, "Certainly. What specifically would you like to know?" Remember Goober in the chapter about the sound bite? Although he anticipated this question, he didn't prepare for it. Now he must be ready to respond instantly. We know where that will go. You won't do that.

Time out. What I'm going to teach you here are the strategy and tactics necessary to manage the interview. As long as the hiring manager is in charge, you're flying blind. I'm going to give you the tools to turn the interview into a conversation. An interview is adversarial. A conversation develops relationships. Many people who hear me talk about this for the first time either start quivering in fear or totally misunderstand, thinking I advocate being aggressive to the point that the hiring manager will be offended, and will take it out on them. Not so. Goober would use a blunt instrument to beat the hiring manager into submission. Unlike him, but much like the doctor, you will have a good, low key, bedside manner, and you will develop a relationship.

This is where you begin to leave Goober in the dust. This is where you use the sound bite—that 60-second positioning statement that you've been practicing.

"Well, I have over ten years' experience in . . ."

Now, if your interviewer didn't know what he was doing when he said, "Tell me about yourself," this is good stuff. If he did know what he was doing, this is exactly what he's hoping for.

Let's take a minute to discuss a critical element of this process.

If "Tell me about yourself" isn't the first question in the interview, the sound bite isn't the first answer!

This may seem like common sense to you, but it isn't to Goober.

Goober has guessed the hiring manager will lead off with "tell me about yourself," and he is excitedly waiting in ambush with the sound bite ready so he can stun the manager with his great expertise. But that isn't how the manager starts. He asks Goober to tell him what he does in his current job.

Boo-yah! Goober springs the trap! "I'd be happy to," he says, "let me just say that I have over 10 years' experience in blah, blah, blah."

The manager's stunned all right. That isn't what he asked. Now he's sitting back in wonder at Goober's apparent inability to understand simple English. In reaction to the manager's look of astonishment, little beads of perspiration are beginning to appear on Goober's forehead.

What you will do is answer the question, and follow with, "You know, if you could give me a little better sense of the working environment, the kinds of challenges I'd face, what you expect of the person you hire, I think I could do a better job of answering your questions. That would give me a context to work in to make my answers more relevant."

If "Tell me about yourself" isn't the first question in the interview, it is highly unlikely that you will use the sound bite at all in the interview. You may, on occasion, find yourself breaking it up into pieces and using selected pieces in the interview, and that's fine. But don't force it in where it isn't appropriate. The fact that you've got a weapon doesn't mean you have to pull the trigger.

Let's get back to the interview.

So, you're sitting in the hiring manager's office, he's said, "Tell me about yourself," and you've responded with the sound bite. Now it's his turn to talk again. Think he might ask a question? He's still got 19 left. Sweat is beginning to stain the neck of Goober's shirt, but not yours, because you know what to do.

After the sound bite, and before the manager can get to the next question, you will say, "You know, if you could give me a little better sense of the working environment, the kinds of challenges I'd face, what you expect of the person you hire, I think I could do a better job of answering your questions. That would give me a context to work in to make my answers more relevant."

Yes, once you have finished the sound bite, keep talking— ask a question. Take a breath if you must, but do it quickly, and keep moving.

Now you've stopped talking, it's his turn to talk, and he has been asked for information. He may give it. If he does, now you're in the right roles. Keep asking until you know what the situation is, what the problems are.

If you're interviewing with a pro, however, he'll say, "No problem, we'll get to that. First I'd like to learn a little more about you." So that didn't work.

Before we move on, let's talk about the question you ask. What you ask is up to you, of course. But I'm partial to "the working environment, the challenges involved, and your expectations." Why? Because, if you tell me those three things, I can tell you in a heartbeat if I'm the right person. But again, it's up to you.

## Fallback #1

But here we have a problem, because asking a question didn't work on the hiring manager. So, your first fallback is to answer a question with a question.

It's likely the next question will be a behavioral one: "Tell me about a time when you had a situation like this, tell me what you did about it, and what the result was." Note that this is an experience-based question, rather than the ability-based question he should be asking.

Your answer will be, "Well, not too long ago I had a situation that I think was very much like that. The situation was blah, blah, blah. I did this, that, and the other, and I got this result. Now, help me. How does the situation that I just described relate to your situation here?" This is where you will really be glad you spent so much time documenting success.

Do not ask, "Does this relate . . .?" Ask, "How does this relate . . .?" It doesn't take much more brain power to say, "It doesn't," than it does to say, "No." But it does take a little bit more.

Michael Phelps, the Olympic swimmer, got one of his gold medals by winning a race by one one-hundredth of a second. The point here is that you don't have to be perfect. But you do have to be one one-hundredth of a second better than everyone else. What I'm trying to do with this book is give you as many one one-hundredths as possible.

Now the manager has been asked for information, so he may give it. If he does, you're in the right roles. Keep asking questions!

But the pro will say, "I just told you—we'll get to that." So you can't try asking a question again.

Your next fallback is to pause the interview.

## Fallback #2

"You know, I'd be happy to answer just about any question you might have. Based on the little that I know about this job, I think I'm qualified; and I certainly don't mind talking about myself. But the fact is that I'm truly ignorant about your situation here, the specific needs you have, what there is in my background that applies. In that kind of ignorance, I could leave out critical information, and then we both lose." This isn't saying you didn't research the company—we'll get to that in a little while. Neither ads nor the position descriptions from which they spring say anything at all about problems. This will leave you ignorant of what the employer expects of you going into the interview.

Now, there are two hooks in what you say. The first is, "Then we both lose." You will remember that losing was not an option in the manager's mind coming into the interview. But there you are, sitting there comfortably and politely telling him that, not only is it an option, he's heading in that direction right now! Well, he doesn't want to lose. Your comment goes right in under the radar, and lodges in the manager's unconscious.

The second hook is the logic of what you're saying, which, in a nice way, is, "If you won't tell me what the job is, how can I even know whether I'm qualified or not, much less tell you."

That's difficult logic to get past. The only way he knows to do it is to just trash it.

He might say, "I understand that. What you need to understand is that this is my interview, and we're going to do this my way!" This is actually a quote. A hiring manager said these words to a client of mine in an interview.

## Fallback #3

Last fallback—terminate the interview. Yes, I know, you think I'm crazy. Don't leave yet. Read on.

"You know, I think I'm probably not the person you're looking for. I appreciate the opportunity to be here, I hope you find the right person, but I don't think I'm the one. Have a nice day." This is how my client responded to the manager.

Leave, go find your interviewer's boss and replace him, because the interviewer is Goober's uncle. And his boss knows it—he's had to deal with the complaints of the people who work for him. If he's so bent on controlling this interview that he'll go to that extent, what do you think he's like to work for? You don't want to be there.

My client stood up to leave but didn't make it to the hiring manager's door before the manager called him back, they started over, they did it the client's way, and he got the offer. Wisely, he turned it down.

Goober, the student-child, could never terminate an interview. He'll just sit there, sweat running down his face, and get hammered for the next half hour.

I don't care who you are. I've worked with everyone from the Chairman of the Board to the guy who dumps the trash at night. When you're looking for a job, self-confidence is your biggest challenge. So you walk into your interviewer's office with a little bit of it, and he beats on you for 45 minutes. Tell me where your self-confidence is now when you're walking out of the door. It's nowhere.

Terminate the interview. Do it very politely, do it nicely, but do it and leave, self-confidence intact.

What I've done here is give you the worst possible outcome for each step in the interview.

If talk about terminating interviews makes you nervous, perhaps this will help. Out of the thousands of clients that I've worked with over the years, the one I just told you about above is the only one I know of who has terminated an interview after we worked on interviewing. It didn't turn out badly for him.

The fact is that somewhere in this process the other person starts talking, and almost always it's right up front. You ask them to tell you about the work, their expectations of the person they hire, and they do! Now you're asking the questions, and they're answering them, and you're in the right roles.

Once you have asked enough questions, you will understand the issues involved, the problems. At this point you will know whether you're the right person for the job or not.

## The Close, Part 1

If you're not, tell them so. "You know, based on what you're telling me, I think I'm probably not the right person for this job."

It's a funny thing. I ask clients who have hired people if they have ever heard those words in an interview. It's very unusual for someone to say yes. You know why? Because everyone in America, taking their cue from Goober, was perfect for the job. It's the student-child. "I'll be good! Hire me. Please?"

It's also why so many hiring managers are trying to kill their candidates.

But you are not Goober.

Having told him that you're not the one he's looking for, turn the hiring manager into a resource. "Let me explain what I'm trying to accomplish, and maybe there's someone here in the company, or maybe elsewhere in the industry, you could refer me to."

They'll do it out of gratitude! They don't have to kill you.

Goober, having failed to convince the manager that he was perfectly qualified for a job that he knew he was not, will slink out of the manager's office exhausted, and head for the nearest bar to drown his sorrows. You will stride out of the manager's office with confidence, and the names of other people you can talk further with in your search.

Before we talk about what to do if you're the right person for the job, let's stop for a moment. I expect you're normal, so when I started talking about terminating the interview, you started getting nervous. Let me stress that termination of an interview is extreme and is only done when all other means of problem discovery are exhausted. Moreover, so far as I know, terminating the interview and walking out has only occurred once out of countless interviews. I believe that you don't have to give it any thought after reading this, but you do have to know what to do if the situation presents itself.

## The Close, Part 2

So, if you are the right person, you'll know that too. And you will say, "You know, I think I can help you with that. Let me explain why." And the reason you'll use those words is because they make people feel relief.

Years ago, I did an informal survey. Of clients who said they had hired consultants, I would ask, "When you had explained your problem to the consultant, did the consultant say, "I believe we can help you with that?" Almost everyone said yes.

I would ask those people, "How did you feel when you heard those words?"

Out of all the people I asked, and I would guess it was about forty, everyone but one said either "relieved" or "relief." And the one who didn't, said, "Much better," which sounds like relief to me.

People are programmed to feel relief when they hear those words, so use them. "I think I can help you with that. Let me explain why." And you can explain why because you know what the issues are, and you know who you are.

That is being the consultant/doctor.

What I have done here is to give you a process (tactics) to turn the interview around (strategy). Sure the hiring manager is looking for the best candidate, but you are looking for the best employer, and that will be very difficult to do by just sitting there trying to answer the hiring manager's questions.

By the same token, you must recognize that, if the interview progresses through each of the fallback stages I've taught you, the potential for chemistry, the most important factor in the interview, erodes with each fallback. However, I have never been told by a client that using this process alienated a person with whom they interviewed.

## "So, How Much Money Do You Want?"

Everyone knows you don't talk about money in the interview. When I ask clients, "Why don't you want to talk about money?" I get two answers: "I don't want to name a figure that's too high and get ruled out," or, "I don't want to name a figure that's too low and either get ruled out, or leave money on the table." They're both valid. But there's a bigger reason.

Have you ever bought a car from a car dealer? Let's go buy a car today.

In my head, I've got a vision of car.

Jaguar. XKR. Convertible. Emerald Fire green. Tan interior. Mega sound system.

Now, in my head I also have a vision of what I'll pay for this car. That's an $80,000 car, minimum. I've done my homework. I'm not going to get taken on that car.

So, I go visit the local Jaguar dealer and go inside, where I'm greeted by the sales representative.

I admit to the sales guy that I'm looking for an XKR convertible, etc., and he says, "Come with me for just a minute." And out the back door we go.

And there it is. Alone on the lot. Golden shaft of sunlight shining down upon it. It glints off the silver jaguar on the hood.

It's a convertible. Emerald fire green. Metallic emerald fire green.

I go to it and bend over to look at the instruments, and the aroma of leather wafts past my nose.

The sales guy hands me the key, and I sit in the driver's seat. It just sighs, "Gotcha'."

I turn the key, and it starts immediately. I take it out on the road. Heads turn as I pass.

This is cool. Very, very cool.

Now, do you think I might be persuaded to pay a dollar or two more for *that* Jaguar than the one that was in my head when I walked into the dealership?

Here's an interesting statistic. The next time you go to a car dealership, touch the car. That's all you have to do. You have just increased the odds that you'll buy it by 500 percent.

So, what does that have to do with "How much money do you want?"

Do you think you might be worth more to the hiring manager as the solution to his problem than you are as one of several candidates for employment?

At the end of the interview, the hiring manager has found, to his delight, that you're great for this job. But he has also discovered, to his profound relief, that you have solved the very problem that will cause him to lose his job in the next 90 days if he doesn't get it fixed. How much will he pay now?

What's a career worth?

Do you think that he might even rewrite the job description to get more money if he has to? Of course. I've seen that happen dozens, maybe hundreds of times!

But if you told him what you wanted, and you're in his salary range, he doesn't have to. You just left money on the table.

You never, ever talk about money in the interview.

So how do you not talk about money?

First, by not giving up your right to not talk about it.

Goober answers the money question out of fear. Having given the interviewer power and authority over him when he walked into his office, he is now afraid to anger him by not answering the question.

Tell me one other negotiation you would go into by telling someone what your bottom line was. I can't think of one. Then why would you do it in one of your most important negotiations? It makes no sense.

The best answer I've ever gotten to the money question was when I was doing an interview workshop, and I was role-playing with a nice lady. I asked her in my most intimidating employer's voice, "So how much money do you want?" And her face just lit up! She got this warm, motherly smile on her face and said, "I can't answer that question. If I name a figure that's too high, you won't hire me! And if I name a figure that's too low, I'll leave money on the table. I can't tell you that!"

Well. Where can you go with that answer? Nowhere. It was perfect. It was true, and it was said with a warm, motherly smile.

Well, being male, I have trouble with the warm, motherly smile part, but if I were asked how much I want I would ask, "What is the salary range for the job?" Then, no matter what the range is, "I understand. Let's keep talking." That has worked for a lot of clients. My wise guy answer is, "You know, probably more than you want to pay. Everyone I ever hired wanted more than I wanted to pay. Shoot, I figure now it's my turn! Seriously though, we don't even know we have a good match yet. Let's just shelve money as an issue. We can come back to that when we know we have a good match." That has also worked for a lot of clients.

But the fact is there is no magic bullet at this point in the interview. If a hiring manager wants to hang the interview on the question, "How much money do you want," he can do it. He can terminate the interview if you won't tell him.

And if he does that, rejoice. You've just found one more idiot you don't have to work for. If he's willing to make a hiring decision by terminating the interview because you won't tell him how much you want, when you both know that's a negotiation, how stupid is he?

Some people just like to play hardball. They'll say something like, "You have to understand that we're not going any farther in this interview until we talk about money. I don't want to waste my time if you want too much."

Respond with, "Well, I'm sorry to hear that. I had hoped to hear more about the job. I charge for my work based on the work, and we haven't really discussed that yet."

And then, if the hiring manager wants to terminate the interview, let him, and rejoice as you leave. You have just been saved from a miserable experience.

One answer you absolutely cannot give is one that Goober thinks is cool: "Are you offering me a job?"

This answer, usually accompanied by a smirk, is one I've had to deal with repeatedly. My response is, with an absolutely deadpan facial expression, "No."

Now it's Goober's turn to talk. What is he going to say?

More importantly, his wise-guy answer has just cost him about 10 points in the interview. I don't need jokers on my team.

But now we get to the real heart of the matter. As I said, there is no magic bullet. There is no magic phrase you can utter that will cause the interviewer to forget that he asked the question.

The good news is that the words may not be as important as your manner of delivery. Our understanding or acceptance of what others say is based only seven percent on the words they use, 33 percent on their tone of voice, and 60 percent on their body language. I learned this in a marriage seminar, and it applies here, too. The parallels between hiring and marriage are enormous.

The hiring manager can ask, "How much money do you want?" And if you're sitting there comfortably, smiling nicely, you can tell him politely to take a leap and he won't get upset, but I don't recommend that.

You never talk about money, either how much you want, or how much you make or made. It's none of their business.

Turn it around on them: "Gee, I got paid in my last job to do some things that you don't want me doing here. And by the same token, you're going to pay me to do some things I didn't have to do there. There's not a really close parallel here. More to the point, I don't want to be valued by you based on my value to someone else. If I thought that were enough, I probably wouldn't be here right now. I want to be valued by you based on my value to you. What would you say that is?"

It's amazing how many people will talk about money if you won't. They'll say, "How much money do you want," and you won't tell them. And then they'll say, "Well, the range for the job is this."

And you'll say, "I understand." You're not saying you'll take it. You're just saying you understand that's what the range is. Never talk about money. Remember, you're always worth more as the last one standing.

### "What Are Your Strengths?"

Now you know what the next question is going to be. "What are your weaknesses?"

I don't believe there is anyone who has ever been interviewed who doesn't know they'll be asked the strength and weakness questions. But nobody gets ready for it. It's amazing.

I'm going to give you a way to answer the strength and weakness questions in a way that will score maximum points, no matter how they're asked, no matter what the application.

First, definitions.

A strength is an aspect of your character or personality that is more fully developed in you than in those around you. Strengths are universal. Everyone has them. They are plural. Everyone has more than one.

You refer to a strength in a three-step process:

---

*Step 1: Name the strength;*
*Step 2: Give an example from work;*
*Step 3: Tell the interviewer what others, preferably a boss—if not a boss, then preferably a client—said about your strength.*

---

"I suppose one strength would be my flexibility. I worked for a time for a start-up government consulting firm, where my title was Administrative Manager, but my real role in the company was fire chief. The CEO told me on my first day on the job that, while he expected me to manage the administrative affairs of the company, that was nowhere near a full-time job. What he really wanted me to do was to walk around looking for problems.

Well, we were a venture capital start-up. All we had were problems. My job was to juggle the crises until we could get the right technical, or legal, or financial talent involved. The CEO told me once that the only reason I was in that job was my ability to handle more than one thing at a time without dropping something."

Now, is flexibility a strength of mine? Sure. Are you going to argue with the CEO? I don't think so.

You must have three strengths. Now for weaknesses.

### "What Are Your Weaknesses?"

A weakness is an aspect of your character or personality that needs work. They are also universal. Every person on the planet has weaknesses. They are also plural. Everyone has more than one.

Trying to pass yourself off as the first human being without any weaknesses, as Goober would do, is strategically unsound.

Nor can you talk about them as though they are really hidden strengths. Everyone has read that book.

You must own your weaknesses.

You also discuss your weaknesses in a three-step process, slightly different from the strengths.

---

*Step 1: "I have a tendency to . . .," or, "I've been told in the past that I . . ."*
*Step 2: Give an example from work.*
*Step 3: "I have had to learn to . . . to keep it from continuing to get me in trouble."*

---

Now, weaknesses are interesting things. Goober would rather go out and lick the parking lot than talk about weaknesses in an interview, and he'll go to amazing lengths to avoid it, including denying the ones he just said he had.

Goober has a real problem with this. He'll get through steps one and two with no problem. Then he'll start step three with the word "but," invalidating steps one and two. Or he'll say, "I've overcome this by . . .." Well, if you've overcome it, it's not a weakness, is it? Goober, why are you telling me this, you idiot?

In fact, no one overcomes weaknesses. Just like strengths, you have them with you forever. On a good day, you can manage a few of them. This is all about weakness management.

"I suppose there are times when I tend to be somewhat indecisive. When I was at the consulting firm that I mentioned earlier, I got in serious trouble on a major project deadline because I put off a couple of critical decisions much longer than I ever should have.

"I've just had to learn to tie my life to a schedule. I don't enjoy it, but I know what happens when I don't. Now it's electronic. Everything goes into the iPhone, not just birthdays and grocery lists. Projects, timelines, checkpoints—just to keep that from continuing to get me in trouble. For a while, if I had lost my iPhone, I'd have been dead meat, but now I've got it backed up in Google."

Now, is indecisiveness a weakness of mine? Sure. Will it be a problem for you, Mr. Employer? Not if I have my iPhone. And Google.

I'm owning the weakness but explaining how I manage it. But don't use the word manage. Let them think of it.

You should have three weaknesses.

"So, Goober, what are your strengths?"

"Well, thank you for asking, I have three strengths, first is this, second is this, blah blah blah."

Goober just shot himself in the foot. The hiring manager knows without question that Goober's response is scripted, memorized, and rehearsed, and he believes none of it.

Actually, your answer should be scripted, memorized, and rehearsed. But it shouldn't sound like it. Shakespeare said all the world's a stage. He was right, and one of the most important stages is the employment interview.

So, pause. Think. Look up. Everyone in history who thought about strengths looked up. I don't know if they think they're written on the ceiling or if they're appealing to the heavens, but everyone does it, so you do it. Look up.

You should look up and to the right. Body language experts say that when you look up and to the right, you are phrasing what you are about to say. If you look up and to the left, you are about to lie. While I don't really buy into that, it doesn't matter much what I think. It matters what the person you're interviewing with thinks.

"I suppose one strength would be my flexibility; blah, blah, blah."

Pause. Let them ask a question; let them make a comment, let them move on if they want.

If they don't, pause. Think a while longer.

"I guess another would be blah, blah, blah."

Pause longer.

"I guess a third (emphasis on *third*) would be blah, blah."

If you get through three of those, they'll move on.

Some will move on after the first. Most will move on after the second. There is no one in America who won't move on after the third. You have used up lots of time, you've been very thorough, and the hiring manager is thinking, "Please, don't tell me another!"

Now, you must have three weaknesses, but you only give them one.

What are your weaknesses?

Pause.

Look down. People who are thinking about weaknesses look down. Shame.

"I suppose I have a tendency at times to blah, blah, blah."

Pause.

And just keep right on pausing.

If you can't stand the silence any longer, just smile and ask, "Was there something else?"

Silence is Goober's worst nightmare. He will say *anything* to fill that dreadful silence.

Most people seem terrified of silence in an interview, and rush to fill it, frequently talking too much or saying the wrong thing. But, as a tactic, silence is neutral. Either side can use it— you use it when you're talking about weaknesses.

What are your weaknesses?

Pause. Think. Look down. Give them one, and stop talking. If they want another one, they'll let you know.

If they do, pause longer. Think. Give them another one. Then be quiet. If they want another, they'll ask. Make them ask.

You'll hardly ever get to three that way. You used as much time talking about two weaknesses as you did with three strengths, and that was a lot.

Now, here's the kicker. If you tell me your strength is flexibility, you had better tell me that your weakness is indecisiveness. How do you think you got so good at being flexible? Flip any strength over and you will find an equivalent weakness. Here are some examples:

- Easy to talk with vs needing to be the center of attention
- Appreciate excellence vs unaccepting of others
- Creative vs overlooking key facts
- Hard-driving vs arrogant
- Objective vs unemotional

- Spontaneous vs impulsive

Goober will say that his strength is flexibility, and his weakness is that he's a perfectionist. These don't fit together. Strengths and weaknesses are opposite sides of the same coin. By the way, never say you're a perfectionist. That's what people say in hopes that you will think they'll do a great job. The concept is talking about a weakness as though it's really a hidden strength. Goober will have a tough time getting a job using this tactic. It is really easy to see through, and has no credibility.

The good news is that there isn't a person in 500 out there who really understands that strengths and weaknesses are opposites, or is thinking about it during the interview, but we all have a sense of "rightness."

If you tell me that your strength is flexibility and your weakness is indecisiveness, those two words circle around to the back of my head and click together, and I say, "Oh, right." And you get a point. I may not even realize I'm giving you the point, but I'm doing it.

So, you must have three strengths and three weaknesses, and they must relate to each other.

Let's consider another aspect of the interview for a moment.

## Preparing For The Interview

When I was about 10 years old, my father taught me how to play chess, and being the kind of guy he was, he saw no reason to lighten up on a 10-year-old. It took me two years to beat him.

On that day, as he was setting up the chess board, I was lacing up my sneakers and thinking, "Here we go again! He's going to beat me." Then I thought, "The only way I have a chance to win is to evaluate every possible move, and every possible consequence of every possible move—every move, his and mine."

I won that day and never lost to him again. (He did walk away from a few four-hour chess matches though.)

What does that have to do with interview preparation?

You must approach the job interview from the standpoint of the hiring manager. You know something about the position for which you're interviewing, or you wouldn't have gotten the interview. Put yourself in the mind of the hiring manager and ask yourself every question you would ask as the hiring manager. Then answer every question, and in the interview, have your answers ready. Remember—it is fine to appear to think in an interview, but it is not fine to have to think. It's too late for that.

Goober would not do this. It's too much trouble. His thought is, "I'll go in there, the hiring manager will ask me some questions, I'll answer them, and I'm outta there." You won't be like Goober. An interview is like a military operation. Every aspect is planned, as is what to do when the unexpected occurs. Remember Eisenhower's words at the beginning of Chapter 5.

Obviously, it would help you to know as much about the company and the job as possible before you interview. Ask for a copy of the position description, if there is one. Remember though, it isn't really the duties and responsibilities you'll read about that are important. It's the *need*. And you'll most likely have to intuit the needs in a job description.

This brings up another point.

There has been a great deal written about the need for you to do research on the company you're interviewing with, so you can appear knowledgeable in the interview. Impress them with your keen understanding of their business.

Even Goober knows this. So he reads up on everything he can about the company, and at a point in the interview when he wants to look particularly brilliant, says to the hiring manager, "I happen to know that Megacorp is doing blah, blah, and blah."

I used to get this all the time when I was a corporate recruiter. I have no problem with doing research on the company. You must to be a viable candidate. What I *do* have a problem with is Goober's need to show that he's special, because he did some research. All too often, the special knowledge that Goober was claiming was either something the company stopped doing six months before or was so commonly known that he got no more points for it than for knowing the name of the company.

So now how smart does Goober look?

You won't be like Goober. You will do the research, and then, in the interview, you will confirm what you've learned.

"In doing research on the company, I read that ABC was the case. How accurate is that?"

This tells the interviewer that you've done the research, and the effect is one of interest in the company, as opposed to a need to show off.

Okay. At the beginning of this chapter, we abused the student-child pretty thoroughly. Maybe you enjoyed some of Goober's antics. Maybe you don't think the student-child exists. Let's look at an example from real life.

My wife and I dated for two and a half years (I was her boss at the time; I don't recommend that.). During that time, we broke up six times. She did it every time. Today she says it wasn't that many, but I was there. (Besides, who's more likely to remember—the breaker, or the breakee?)

She did it because everywhere she looked, there I was. "I'll be good! You'll like me!" She was dating the student-child.

About the fourth time we broke up, she said (and this is a quote), "You are choking me. I need some space. Please, give me some space." Perhaps, if you are female, you can relate.

I responded, "Sure, no problem. You want to have dinner Friday night?" I figured that, if I'm there, no one else can be there. If you're male, maybe you've tried that strategy. The assumption is true, but it doesn't work.

On October 4th, 1978, I asked her to marry me. She said, "I'll let you know."

A few days later, she said, "No. I'd like to be your friend." So, as the student-child, I tried to look at it logically. "On the one hand, we have 'friend.' On the other hand, we have . . . *nothing*! Okay, friend. Sure. Friend's good. Let's do friend."

As friends, we happened to be together on the Sunday afternoon of George Washington's Birthday weekend, 1979, when the Washington, D.C., area was getting history's second biggest snowstorm. There was no way we'd be getting back to the office soon. I have no idea what we were talking about when, out of the blue, I found myself saying to her, "You know, when we do get back to the office, I'm going to resign. I don't know where I'll go, but I'll figure it out. What you need to know is that I'm going this way. If you go this way too, I'm going faster. I don't want to be your friend." And then, inspiration struck.

"You know, as I see it," I said, "you have two choices. You could marry me, or you could get out of my life. If I were you, I think I'd marry me. But it's your choice. I'm comfortable either way."

Three hours later we were engaged. As of this writing, we've been married for forty years. I think we'll keep going.

Here's the point. For two and a half years she was running away from the student-child. The hour I gained independence, she turned around.

Think for a moment about employment interviews you have had. It isn't uncommon to have had an interview in which you realized, early in the interview, that you didn't want the job. Guess who the hiring manager wanted? You, of course. Why? Because the moment you realized that you didn't care about the outcome, you relaxed. The student-child slunk away and hid.

The student-child lurks in everyone to some degree or other, waiting to appear at the worst possible moment in the interview. You need to replace the student-child with the consultant in the interview. You also need to realize that you do not need *this* job. Yes, you do need a job, but you don't need this job. The moment you decide you need this job, the student-child will take over, and you will be lost. Your understanding and acceptance of this is critical to success in the search.

Let's wrap this up. Here's your challenge.

For as long as you have been working, you have been part of the American job culture, and that culture has taught you every day that when you walk into the interview as the candidate for employment, you're the student-child. For a very short time now, I've been telling you that you aren't.

This calls for a bit of mind renewal. If going through the achievement validation in Chapter 2 didn't help with that, take another look at it. You have done some pretty cool things in your life. It's also pretty comforting to realize that your competition is Goober.

*Be the consultant.*

## Summary

This chapter has been all about winning the interview:

1. You are the doctor or consultant, not the student child.
2. There is a process, with fallbacks, for managing the interview.
3. How to answer, "Tell me about yourself."
4. How to answer the money questions.
5. How to relate strengths and weaknesses.
6. Preparing for the interview.

# Chapter 8
# Negotiating

> *Let us never negotiate out of fear.*
> *But let us never fear to negotiate.*
> **– John F. Kennedy**

We established earlier that you don't talk about money in the interview. So when do you talk about money? Once you have an offer.

But when do you start negotiating?

When you and the person who could hire you first lay eyes on each other. Negotiating is about a whole lot more than money.

Let's talk about first impressions.

Studies have shown that within the first five seconds of our laying eyes on each other I will have made a judgment about you—not a hiring judgment, but a positive or negative judgment. That judgment will not change for the next three hours, no matter what you do. If it is positive, you can dance on my desktop, and I'll think that's creative. If it's negative, you have an uphill climb—nothing you do for the next three hours will change it. Most interviews don't last that long.

Moreover, a sizeable percentage of the population, upon meeting someone in a gray or gray pinstripe suit, white shirt, red or gold tie, and black wingtip shoes, ascribes more success and power to that person than they should, because many people of power and influence dress this way. While it doesn't seem to normally be the entrepreneurial style, it is most often the style of finance, big business, and politics. As it is said, Steve Jobs notwithstanding, "Clothes make the man." And the woman, too.

This is all about corporate camouflage. Whether you are male or female, this is not about making a fashion statement. You are making a *business* statement. The business statement is always conservative. Think of stores like Brooks Brothers, Jos. Banks, Talbot's—stores that sell conservative clothes. If that doesn't help, watch what the country's senior political leaders wear on television. The power brokers all wear what I'm talking about.

All that said, you need to know that the type of industry you're looking at, and the geopolitical area in which you live, impact clothing decisions as well. Different industries and geographical areas have different standards of dress. If you don't know the rules of dress to start with, a little research will pay big dividends. Take a close look at the people who work in that field or area—what camouflage are they wearing? Then do likewise. A note in passing—it's always easy to remove a tie or jacket, but it's really hard to put them on if you don't have them.

So, if you are wearing corporate camo, you're home free, right?

Not exactly. What about the handshake?

Your mom was right—firm handshake, look 'em in the eye.

First, the handshake. Earlier I mentioned that I had worked with a client who had been a professional football player. When he shook your hand, his grip was about one click past comfortable, and you knew there were as many clicks more available as he wanted to exert.

Not good. Neither is pumping the person's arm so hard that you give the impression of jacking up a car.

Grab the whole hand—not just the fingers—and grip firmly—not in a vise, pumping the hand—not the arm—gently once or twice.

Then there is the opposite problem—the dead fish handshake. It is even worse than the vise grip.

As to looking them in the eye, in our culture, looking down when meeting or talking with someone is a sign of extreme weakness, and, coupled with the dead fish handshake, will end your candidacy before you've even had a chance to say anything more than hello.

Looking elsewhere is equally bad. I once worked for a guy who never looked at you when he spoke to you. He always looked over your left shoulder. It was very disconcerting. It made you wonder if there was a train coming up fast from behind

There is another aspect to this.

You may have heard that the job search is a sales process, and you're the product. If you haven't yet, you can be certain that you will.

I believe that statement has ruined more job searches than any other you may hear.

Think about it. What do you think of when you hear the word "product?" An appliance—a toaster or blender, perhaps.

What appliances do you buy? The nice, shiny ones.

So if you're the product, you need to be a nice, shiny product that someone will want to buy.

This *immediately* puts you in a subservient role to the buyer—the hiring manager; and out pops the student-child I told you about in the chapter on interviewing.

This truly is a sales process, but you are not the product.

---

*The skills, abilities, and positive qualities you offer an employer are the product.*

---

You can be wearing the absolute best that Brooks Brothers has to offer, but if you're the product, you're in trouble. You will approach the decision maker from an inferior position, rather than as the consultant, and you will surely lose the negotiation.

You must be the consultant!

Now, spending all this time talking about handshakes, clothes, and appliances may seem a bit much, but you must remember that my first impression of you won't go away for three hours. If I judge you to be squared away, successful, and personable, we're off to a very good start, and you're doing well in our negotiation. If I don't, well, good luck.

Let's fast forward. Now, you've got the offer.

Do you accept? Reject? How?

Never accept or reject an offer on the spot. I have a friend who says, "Nobody makes you their best offer. They make you the offer they hope you'll accept." This is absolute truth in my experience.

Before you can make a reasonable judgment regarding the quality of the offer, there are things you must know.

Do you already have a firm understanding of what will be expected of you on the job? Do you know what success looks like?

Do you understand the corporate culture? Does it suit you?

What is your relationship with your potential boss? What about that person's boss? Team members?

What about benefits?

What about additional perks that might be available?

What about an employment contract or separation agreement?

By this point in the process, you should already have a firm understanding of the job, your boss's management style, the culture, etc. If you don't, you don't have much time to do it now. Opportunities for error loom large at this point.

Let's say you've been thorough, and have all the work-related information you need to make a valid decision.

What about benefits?

Here is a list of some of the things you need to know about:

- Vacation—how much, when, does it carry over?
- Sick leave—how much, when, does it carry over?
- Personal leave—how much, when?
- Health coverage—what is it, who pays for how much, when?
- Life insurance—how much, who pays, is more available? At what cost?
- Disability insurance—short term? Long term? How much, what is the cost?
- ESOP (employee stock ownership plan)—available? How does it work?
- Retirement—how much? How does vesting work?

- Thrift and savings plan—who invests, how much, how does it work?
- 401(k)—who invests, how much, how does vesting work?
- Stock ownership—how much, when, is more available?
- Other equity or cash programs—available? How do they work?
- Tuition assistance? How much? What is the employee commitment?
- Relocation assistance (if an issue)?
- Moving allowance or reimbursement?
- What moving expenses are covered?
- What about assistance in sale of house?
- Realtor fees?
- Closing costs?
- Will the company buy the house?
- Temporary living expenses?
- How much?
- How long?
- Where?
- Bridge loan for new house purchase?
- Advance house-hunting trip(s) for family?
- How long to relocate?
- Performance evaluations—how often, how done?
- Salary action—when, based on merit, cost of living, both?
- Average salary increase last year
- Average increase projected for this year
- Promotion—how soon available?
- How long to apply for other jobs internally?

- There could be other benefit and/or procedure issues as well.

These are all things you need to know about and understand before you can negotiate dollars, but it isn't an exhaustive list. There may well be other items. If you don't ask, you won't know.

Now, to the money.

People get nervous about negotiating once the offer comes in. Most are afraid to push for greater compensation out of a fear of losing the offer.

In over thirty years of negotiating on behalf of, or working with clients who negotiated, I've only seen offers withdrawn three times because the candidate tried to negotiate. In each instance the offer was a lowball offer. The hiring manager was out to get a bargain if he could, and if he couldn't, he just wouldn't hire. Clearly, the problem wasn't big enough at the point of the offer. While at the time, the retraction of the offer was traumatic to each client, each had significantly higher offers within a very short time.

Understand that if you are getting a job offer, it is because they *want* you. While there are some people who will only make one offer, they are a minority. Most people will try to get you for the least they can pay. It's human nature.

One of the biggest lessons I learned about negotiating was when I worked for a Fortune 500 company. I had worked there for more than a year when another recruiter was hired. It didn't take long to learn that he started at 20 percent more than I was making. Furious, I went to my boss to get an explanation. Embarrassed, he said, "Please don't take what I'm saying the wrong way, but you made your deal."

He was right. My problem wasn't that they paid the other guy more. My problem was what I let them pay me when I accepted the job. It had been a pretty easy hire, starting when my friend, who held the job at the time, called me and said, "I'm moving to another job. If you want mine, I can get you an interview." At the time, I was languishing as a headhunter working pretty much totally on commission. I didn't enjoy the headhunting business, I wasn't really fond of my boss, I really didn't enjoy being on commission, and here was a chance to join bigtime corporate America. I didn't even think to ask what the salary range was, despite talking to my friend, the guy who definitely knew, and could tell me anything I wanted to know. I just said, "You bet!"

When I interviewed, it all went well with his boss, his boss's boss, and the VP of Human Resources, and they were quick to make an offer. They offer actually was somewhat less than I was making, but the opportunity to get out of where I was, and to get a steady paycheck were all I really cared about. I took it on the spot.

I subsequently saw, and took part in hiring new employees at larger salaries than their peers who had been with the company a year or more, but for some reason, was shocked when it happened to me. Here's the point:

---

*You need to make your deal*

---

Our culture does not do a good job of preparing people to negotiate. We only do it for houses, cars, (and everyone hates that process) and jobs.

You want to get the most money you can. Your employer wants to pay the least possible. It seems like a negotiation is in order.

Below is a representation of a typical job offer over the phone.

Let's say you've gotten the phone call; Mr. Big has said, "You're the one we want. We're offering you the job of Supreme Commander. The salary is X."

Your response is to say nothing for five seconds (bite your tongue and count—slowly!). Then repeat the salary with no inflection.

"X."

Stop talking. The next person to speak loses. Remember, silence is your friend.

Mr. Big will now have to speak. He will likely ask if there is a problem with that. You will say, "I don't know that I would call it a problem, but to be honest, I was expecting more than that. Is that the best you can do?"

Mr. Big will respond in one of three ways. He'll say that it is the best they can do, or that he'll have to check, or he'll say, "What did you have in mind?"

If it's the latter, you will say, "I didn't really have a specific figure in mind. But, based on the conversations I've had with others about pay ranges for people like me, that seems a bit low."

Mr. Big will now either stand his ground or see if he can do better. If he stands his ground, you will say, "Well, let me crunch the numbers and talk with my spouse/significant other, and I'll get back to you within 48 hours." (You will get back to Mr. Big in less than 24 hours. The early response will cause him to like you more!)

If Mr. Big must go see if he can come up with more, you will say, "When should I expect to hear from you? Great. If I haven't heard from you by then, I'll give you a call."

Either way, no decision is made during the first phone call.

There are differences in the way you negotiate, depending on whether you are dealing with your future boss or the human resources person.

I had a client who found a company whose need played directly to his strengths. He interviewed with the CEO, who loved him. Then he interviewed with the management team, and with the people he would be working with. They loved him, too.

He was extended an offer of $54,000 by the CFO. Over the course of three phone conversations, the offer increased next to $84,000, and finally to $96,000. He accepted $96,000.

What should you take away from this?

1. People don't make you their best offer. They make you the offer they hope you'll accept.

2. During the entire hiring process, the client above never answered the question, "How much do you want," including during the negotiation. The hiring manager was negotiating with himself. This is what you want. It is the only way to get the maximum compensation from your prospective employer.

3. Money won in the negotiation compounds over time. Money left on the table never comes back.

At the beginning of this chapter, I quoted President Kennedy saying, ". . . let us never fear to negotiate." He was right.

# CHAPTER 9

# The New Job

> *Try not to become a man of success but rather*
> *to become a man of value.*
> **– ALBERT EINSTEIN**

Now you've been successful in the search. Congratulations!

But what have you done for your new employer lately?

As a new hire, you are automatically defined as part of the solution. This is a great and wonderful thing, but beware the tendency to get comfortable basking in the glow of being perceived as the problem solver.

You'd better go solve a problem!

I worked once with a client who had been very successful in Fortune 500 companies. In one conversation he told me, "In every job I've ever had, I sat down with my new boss during my first week of employment and asked three questions. The first is, 'What is expected of me in this job?' and we would establish that. The second is, 'What do I have to do to be promoted?' and we would establish that. The third is, 'What do I have to do to get *you* promoted?'"

Then he said, "In every job I've ever had, my boss got promoted. And every one of them pulled me up behind them."

This fellow got the point.

Don't get the idea that you were hired to fill a vacancy, or because you're a nice person, or even because you are bright, talented, and can help the company in some way.

---

*You were hired because your new boss believes that you will make him or her look good.*

---

By being the new employee, and therefore part of the solution, you have bought a certain amount of time for yourself. Depending on your place in the food chain, you have a window of thirty days to six months to achieve a noticeable victory. A noticeable victory is defined as a significant increase in revenue or reduction in expenses, a process improvement that creates a significant increase in performance, or a major problem solved.

If you can achieve such a victory, you will have cemented your reputation as part of the solution and bought significantly more time in which to solve more problems. If you are not, you will certainly be redefined as part of the problem, and should immediately begin another job search.

Let's discuss how you will succeed, and lend some structure to the process.

## The Achievement Book

Go out and buy a blank book—the kind isn't important, as long as you can write in it. I recognize that this is low-tech. but I don't want you to use a spreadsheet or other electronic means. I'll explain in a minute.

Your assignment—and this assignment lasts until you retire—is to set aside 30 to 60 minutes of quiet time each week, evaluate the past week, and make entries in the following five categories in your book:

1. What you did for your boss during the past week;
2. What you did for the organization during the past week;
3. What you did for the people who work for or with you during the past week;
4. What specific successes you achieved during the past week;
5. What you did for at least one member of your network.

What you did for your boss is what you did to make your boss's job easier, or to enhance your boss's reputation internally or externally. Remember, your job is to make your boss look good!

What you did for the organization is what you did to increase revenue, reduce costs, increase production or efficiency, or to enhance the organization's image as a corporate citizen of the community.

What you did for the people who work for or with you is what you did to make their jobs easier or more fun, or to enhance their careers. This could be anything from bringing in doughnuts to turning around an underperforming employee.

What successes you achieved must show specific results in terms of revenue enhancement, cost reduction, process or staff improvement, problem solving, or customer's perception enhancement. (**Note**: there is always a customer.)

What you did for at least one member of your network is what you did to further establish the relationship. It could be dining with someone, it could be sending a birthday card, or helping someone get another job. There are many possibilities.

"I did my job," is not an acceptable entry for any category. That's where you start.

The fellow who showed me this process said, "If you go three weeks without making an entry, start looking for a job."

Incidentally, if you only pay attention to the first category, the people in #3 will see to it that you fail. If you only focus on #3, the person who is #1 will fire you. You've got to pay attention to all the categories.

Here's the theory. It's time for your annual performance review.

Here is what your boss has done to prepare for the review: nothing. He is vaguely aware that you were there a year ago because it's your annual review. He knows a little more about what was going on six months ago, and is right on top of the last two weeks.

Here is what you have done to prepare: you have religiously made entries in the above categories. You are armed with a year's worth of things you did for your boss, a year's worth of things you did for the organization, and a year's worth of things you did for your fellow employees or direct reports, plus specific, quantified examples of success. And when you pull out your book your boss knows immediately that you've won. Remember, all the world's a stage.

This process netted a client of mine a 40 percent salary increase and a transfer to the only part of the company he knew he wanted to work in. His boss told him at the time that the raise and transfer were due entirely to what he said in his performance evaluation. What he said in his performance evaluation came entirely from his book.

Furthermore, recognize that if you don't feed the network you have built throughout the job search, it will die. Where will you be then, when you need to find another job?

Remember, the whole point of managing your career is to cause the next job to come to you, and to help others.

I believe this process has the potential to make you more money over time than almost anything else you do. But it's a difficult habit to develop, because you can always catch up next week. But if you put it off, next week will never come.

Well, I can't tell you how many clients I've worked with who disappeared shortly after getting a new job, only to reappear six months later saying they had a massive problem and had to look for a new job.

In just about every case, when I asked to see their achievement book, there was none.

You've been through the agony of going through your whole career to find successes to write and talk about. It only makes sense to continue doing it in real time. The documentation process takes no more than 60 minutes per week. Of course, if by Wednesday or Thursday you have no achievements to write about, you'd better start creating some! That, admittedly, takes some effort. But if you make the effort you may be promoted. If you don't, you will suffer Goober's fate.

This is how you must approach your new job, and all subsequent jobs.

You were hired because your new boss believes you can solve a problem or problems that he or she has, and make him or her look good. If you demonstrate that you understand that, and do it, not once, but repeatedly, your future is assured, *if the organization maintains the status quo.*

But that isn't likely. So, while you are busily creating and documenting success on the job, you must also devote time and energy off the job to first solidify and then expand your network.

## The Network

It's time to do some writing, but first you have some prioritizing to do.

You should be able to list all the people you met with during your search. Divide them into two groups: those people you want to maintain contact with and those you don't. You will want to maintain contact with those people you like and/or respect, those who can be of further help to you in the future, those who are prominent in your field or industry, and those whom you like and can help, now or in the future. Those you don't want further contact with are those who are of no future value to you (cold, isn't it?) that you don't like or respect, those who threw you out of their offices, and those you can't remember.

Likely, there will be a middle group of people that you're not sure what to do about. If the "further contact" group consists of twenty or more people, I'd probably put these people in the "no further contact" group. If the number is less than twenty, I'd be tempted to put them in the "further contact" group and let them sort themselves out.

Now it's time to send some cards, but this time you get to select the picture on the front. I had a client who found a picture on the internet of a duck landing in water, and had the picture made into cards. The opening line of the card? "I've landed!" Brilliant!

The cards you send to the people with whom you don't want to stay in touch will tell them:

1. You've accepted a position as (title) at (company);
2. Thanks for their help in your search;
3. That if you can ever be of help to them, they have only to get in touch with you.

The cards you send to those people you want to stay in touch with, hereafter identified as "network affiliates," will tell them:

1. You've accepted a position as (title) at (company);
2. Thanks for their help in the search (if it was significant, be specific);
3. That if you can ever be of help to them, they have only to get in touch with you;
4. That you'd very much like to stay in touch with them;
5. You'll send them a business card as soon as you get them.

This activity should be completed no later than one week after you have accepted your new job.

Your assignment relative to your new network affiliates is to stay in touch, but don't make a pest of yourself.

You should get together at least once every three to six months to catch up—informally. This could be a meal, or just getting together for coffee.

If you see industry, professional, or avocational material that might interest them, send it to them. You should know their interests.

If they're looking for a job, help them.

Introduce them to people you know who might be relevant to them.

There could only be two reasons you find yourself reading this. Either you didn't have a network before you got the book, or you didn't know what to do with it. Now you have one, and you must care for it and feed it, so you don't find yourself repeatedly coming back to this book for remedial job-hunting assistance later. The importance of the achievement book and the network simply cannot be overemphasized.

In more than twenty years of coaching people, I can probably count on two hands the number of clients who have consistently done these things. (By the way, they've been very successful!)

Our friend Goober hates job-hunting so much that when he gets a job, he wants to immediately cast from memory everything to do with his just-completed and oh-so-painful job search.

Here's the problem. Goober will rejoice! Maybe throw a party. He will forget as much as possible about the job search because it was so distasteful, and he will embrace his new job and these wonderful new people who will love him and care for him. And he'll be busy. He'll need to learn the ropes, adjust to a new culture, etc. And ultimately, he'll get comfortable in his job and fall into the trap of complacency. But within three years something will happen. The company will get bought, or buy another company. The technology will change or move offshore. He'll get a new boss who won't recognize Goober's sterling qualities. The company will stop doing what he does. The economy will tank or take off. Some change will occur to cause Goober to have to get another job, and he'll be no better prepared for that job search than he was for the last one, because he didn't document success or feed the network.

The fact is you will never stop looking for a job. Only the intensity and tactics will change. The absolute best time to look for a job is right after you've gotten one.

If you have spare time, go to your boss and ask how you can be of help. Volunteer for projects that might require you to learn new things. Help your teammates.

Identify areas in your new organization in which you might have a future interest. What are they doing? What kinds of challenges do they face? What do you have to learn to be valuable in those areas? Get to know the people in charge. Volunteer to help if you have the time. Build relationships. If you can demonstrate that you are the kind of person who can make those managers look good, who do you think they'll come after when they have a need?

Obviously, this is all predicated on your having already covered your own responsibilities. You had better make sure that your own work is done before you go trotting off to help someone else!

Now is the time to join professional associations if you haven't already done so. Frequently professional or trade associations that you might want to join require corporate membership. Ask if your company will join and pay for you. If they won't, ask if they'll join and let you pay for you. Consider it an investment in your future.

Become active in these organizations. It does you little good to join if you're going to be invisible. Assume a leadership role. Membership chair is always a good one, because you'll meet everyone in the organization.

Now is also the time to start meeting the people who might hire you in other companies. You should always have a target list of companies in which you are interested, and the names of the people in those companies who might ultimately hire you. Get out there and get to know the competition. They'll be impressed. In the chapter on networking, I stressed that your goal was to get your profile into the file that hiring managers keep in their desk drawers, their computers, or their heads. Stay in touch with these people. If they were impressed enough with you to keep your profile, they consider you to be a future pick, so cement the relationship!

Remember, if you are not putting consistent, conscious effort into managing your career, and are just doing your job, you are asking to get whacked.

The search and relationship-building concepts and tools you've gained from this book must be used at least until you retire, move to Florida, put on those plaid pants and sneakers, and go for long walks on the beach. Maybe there, too.

The winds of change are blowing strong. You have got to take notice of them, or you will become irrelevant. While there is probably still a niche market for buggy whip makers, I'll bet it is highly competitive, and you really don't want to depend on that for a living!

The whole concept of career management is that you never stop looking for a job—not necessarily with the effort you have expended in this search, but with the idea of always keeping your eyes open, always being open to new opportunity, always meeting new people, always knowing where the next opportunity lies in the company employing you.

Your next job should come to you when someone with whom you've developed a working relationship calls you and says, "You might want to have a look at what's going on over here."

But for now, you've been successful.

---

*Congratulations!*

---

# About the Author

B ud Whitehouse says he has most likely failed his way to success. Organic chemistry cut short what was to be a brilliant medical career, causing him ultimately to stumble into headhunting. Following that mercifully short experience, he languished in stints as a corporate recruiter, human resources generalist and manager, organization development consultant, and corporate outplacement consultant. While he enjoyed none of these jobs, he learned a great deal from all of them. He has used that knowledge for more than 25 years to help thousands of clients get better jobs, for more money, faster, dramatically improving their careers and lives.

He was born in Washington, DC, and worked in that area for more than 20 years. He currently lives and works in Richmond, Virginia. He and his wife have two grown children and three grandchildren.

## FREE BONUS

# Set Up Your FREE Consultation with Bud!

Thank you for reading When Can You Start? Now it's time to take the next step and get your new career path started on the right foot.

Go to https://whitehouse.coach and you will get immediate access to a FREE consultation. We will set up a time to talk so we can figure out the best next step for you.

Don't wait! Do this right now! Go to https://whitehouse. coach. Once you are there, simply click the Contact link at the top, fill out the form provided, then click the submit button and we will get your free consultation set up right away!

Don't waste another second. Let's set up a time to talk.